wedding wisdom

A Practical Guide to Personalizing Your Wedding

DOREEN WUCKERT

Marriage Officiant for Over 30 Years

◆ FriesenPress

Suite 300 - 990 Fort St
Victoria, BC, V8V 3K2
Canada

www.friesenpress.com

Copyright © 2021 by Doreen Wuckert
First Edition — 2021

All rights reserved.

Edited by Grant Wuckert and Doug Stone

No part of this publication may be reproduced in any form, or by any means, electronic or mechanical, including photocopying, recording, or any information browsing, storage, or retrieval system, without permission in writing from FriesenPress.

ISBN
978-1-5255-9085-6 (Hardcover)
978-1-5255-9084-9 (Paperback)
978-1-5255-9086-3 (eBook)

1. FAMILY & RELATIONSHIPS, MARRIAGE

Distributed to the trade by The Ingram Book Company

"Doreen was a wonderful guide. She helped us to create a one of a kind ceremony. We were thrilled to have her take part in our special day."

— Megan and Gord Wilding

"They say if it rains on your Wedding Day, it means good luck. Well they are right. We asked Doreen Wuckert to officiate my daughter's wedding. That is when the luck began. When it started pouring rain during the outside ceremony, Doreen was so totally relaxed while we found an indoor venue, a small movie theatre. We had the most beautiful and fun 'Popcorn Wedding.'"

— (See anecdote 14) Arlene Stanlake, mother of the bride

TABLE OF CONTENTS

About the Author	vii
Preface	viii
Introduction	x
Explanation of Terms	xii
26 Unusual Anecdotes (Found Throughout the Book)	xiv
Acknowledgments	xvi
Chapter 1: What to Ask Your Partner Before You Get Married	5
Chapter 2: The Marriage Officiant	11
The Role of the Marriage Officiant	*11*
How to Select an Officiant: What to Ask	*11*
The Marriage License	*13*
Meeting with the Officiant	*14*
Applying to be a One-Time Marriage Officiant	*16*
Applying to be a Permanent Marriage Officiant	*16*
Chapter 3: The Marriage Ceremony	24
Requirements	*24*
Typical Marriage Ceremony Outline	*25*
Types of Marriage Ceremonies	*27*
Sample Script of a Traditional Marriage Ceremony	*28*

Chapter 4: Planning the Wedding   38
   Options for 15 Parts of a Wedding   *38*
   Wedding Locations – Free to Expensive   *43*
   11 Precautions to Prevent Things That May Go Wrong   *45*

Chapter 5: Unity Rituals   59

Chapter 6: Sound Advice and Suggestions   67

Chapter 7: Marriage Testimonies: More Than
50 Years of Retrospection   76
   Wendy's Testimony   *76*
   Kenn's Testimony   *79*
   Darlene's Testimony   *82*
   Paul's Testimony   *85*
   Gordon's Testimony   *90*
   Doreen's Testimony   *92*

Final Thoughts   95

Appendix 1: Marriage Ceremony Scripts   97

Appendix 2: Suggested Readings for Weddings   121

Appendix 3: Recommended Books   125

ABOUT THE AUTHOR

Doreen Wuckert has been a marriage officiant for more than thirty years. She has officiated hundreds of weddings in English, French, Spanish and Italian. Sometimes she has used three languages at one wedding. She is a language teacher by profession. She currently is a faculty supervisor in the Education Department of the University of Winnipeg. She also works as an interpreter and teaches this subject at the Immigrant Centre of Manitoba. Her other activities include being a yoga and fitness instructor.

Doreen has been married to Grant Wuckert since April 1972. She still enjoys the vicarious thrill of seeing happy couples commit to one another, witnessed by loving family and friends.

PREFACE

Reminiscing with my husband about romantic and humorous experiences we have enjoyed during my thirty-plus years as a marriage officiant, Grant suggested I record my most interesting wedding stories. In writing these unusual anecdotes, I realized that couples often make mistakes because they are not well prepared.

I found little information online or in wedding books on step-by-step approaches for creating a personalized, stress-reduced wedding ceremony where the couple is in control. So I designed and taught a course called Preparing for Marriage – Creating Your Own Wedding Ceremony. With the outline of the course, my students' questions and concerns and my interesting anecdotes, I knew it was time to sit down and write this book.

It has been an interesting process for me to compile not just anecdotes, but ceremonies for all loving couples: straight, same-sex, second marriages, blended families, double marriages, renewal of vows, and a few bilingual samples.

It has been more than satisfying to help couples get ready for one of the most important events of their lives by compiling a list of questions couples should ask one another before marriage. These questions help guard against pitfalls that can harm a loving relationship.

I hope that by reading this book couples develop a confidence, not only in planning their marriage ceremony and wedding, but going forward into a long, healthy and meaningful relationship.

INTRODUCTION

The purpose of this book is to examine, from an experienced marriage officiant's perspective, all aspects of weddings, focusing on the marriage ceremony. I wish to help loving couples prepare for this very special event. Chapter 1, What to Ask Your Marriage Partner Before You Get Married, addresses the importance of each partner being ready for marriage. All couples are included: heterosexual, same sex, gender fluid, etc. Chapter 6 offers suggestions and some sound advice for all loving couples.

Finding a good marriage officiant is important for the ceremony to go smoothly. Suggestions for choosing a good officiant and what to discuss are in Chapter 2, The Marriage Officiant.

Chapter 3, The Marriage Ceremony, explains the heart of a wedding, what its parts are, what is essential and what is not. This chapter presents a typical outline in nine parts, as well as a sample script for a traditional ceremony. Appendix 1 provides scripts for other types of ceremonies, including different spiritual needs, sexual orientations, and languages (French, Spanish and Italian). Appendix 2 provides suggestions for ceremony readings, which are included in most weddings. Appendix 3 lists some helpful books related to marriage, parenthood and life in general.

Weddings I have officiated have generally been romantic and happy. However, there have been unusual situations that have been tense, surprising, tear-jerking, or quirky. This is illustrated throughout the book in twenty-six anecdotes that demonstrate how the officiant must work with a variety of personalities and how the officiant and the couple should be well prepared. Also, the anecdotes are fun.

EXPLANATION OF TERMS

For clarification, six terms should be explained.

1. A <u>marriage</u> is different from a wedding. A marriage is a relationship solemnized (duly performed with formal ceremony) by a marriage officiant.
2. A <u>marriage ceremony</u> is the heart of a wedding. It is a service that solemnizes a marriage. There cannot be a formal marriage without a marriage ceremony. A secular marriage ceremony is usually 15 to 20 minutes long, but may take only a few minutes. Religious marriage ceremonies are usually longer.
3. <u>Wedding</u> is a broader term than marriage ceremony. A wedding includes the marriage ceremony and the entire framework around it, such as location, photography, music and the audience, plus associated celebrations. A wedding generally lasts several hours. However, it need not be longer than the marriage ceremony itself.
4. A <u>marriage officiant</u> is empowered by the government to perform a marriage ceremony. The officiant's main responsibilities are to witness the consent of the intended spouses, validate the marriage and witness the signing of the marriage license.

5. The term <u>marriage commissioner</u> is synonymous with marriage officiant. This book only uses marriage officiant (or officiant for short).
6. <u>Wedding ceremony</u> and <u>marriage ceremony</u> are synonymous.

26 UNUSUAL ANECDOTES (FOUND THROUGHOUT THE BOOK)

Most weddings go quite smoothly. However, of the hundreds of weddings I have officiated, there definitely have been unusual exceptions. The twenty-six anecdotes found throughout the book range from tense, surprising, tear jerking or quirky. The titles, with page numbers, are:

1. Red Shag Carpet / 1
2. Buzz What? / 2
3. The Delusional One / 7
4. Whatever! / 9
5. Wedding Faux Pas / 17
6. Wedding Refused / 18
7. No Marriage License? / 20
8. N.S.F. / 22
9. No Charge / 23
10. The Lost Ring / 32
11. Wedding Theatrics / 33
12. Short and Sweet / 35
13. Same-Sex Marriage / 36
14. Popcorn Wedding / 47
15. Hockey Ceremony #1 (Neighborhood Surprise) / 48
16. Hockey Ceremony #2 (NHL Arena) / 50
17. Are They Really Married? / 51

18. Too Drunk to Listen / 53
19. Time Shift / 55
20. My Error This Time / 57
21. At the Last Minute / 63
22. Marriage Tension / 65
23. Biker Wedding / 66
24. Lights Out / 71
25. Best Wedding Gift / 72
26. Love During COVID-19 / 74

ACKNOWLEDGMENTS

My special thanks to my loving partner of more than fifty years. Grant edited this book and has been a major support since we first met. Doug Stone helped with formatting and editing, and gave good advice. My son, Lance Wuckert, was the IT support for this book. Thank you also to my two grandchildren, Ty and Brooke, who bring me great joy.

Anecdote 1

Red Shag Carpet

A Goth couple showed up at my home. They were both wearing the full black regalia: black shirts, pants, boots, lipstick, hair and nail polish. They wanted to get married…like now. As they entered the living room, she excitedly reacted to our thirty-year-old bright red shag carpet: "How retro!" I told them they would need a marriage license and sent them off to obtain one.

They waited the legal twenty-four hours and were back at my house. Although impulsive, they were serious about getting married. However, they did not have the required two witnesses. My husband, Grant, and a next-door neighbor acted as their witnesses.

After the ceremony, they insisted on having their photos taken on our "retro" red shag carpet, lying on their backs, side by side with arms crossed over their chests. My husband jumped up on the couch to take photos from above. They looked like corpses lying motionless, all in black.

Until death do they part?

Anecdote 2

Buzz What?

It was a blended family wedding ceremony. The bride-to-be was marrying for a second time. She had a son who was about eight years old. I met the couple in advance, but not the son.

During the ceremony, the groom would get down on his knee and tell the boy how much he was looking forward to being his new dad. The couple wanted to include the boy as much as possible. His name would be mentioned several times in the ceremony.

About fifty people were in attendance. The bride came forward with her son. They stood before me as the groom joined them. I proceeded with the ceremony.

The first time I mentioned the boy's name, he mumbled something I did not understand. I continued. Again, when I mentioned the boy's name, he mumbled something. It sounded something like "bis lyre." I proceeded but felt I should find out what he was trying to tell me. I decided if he mumbled something one more time, I would stop the proceedings and ask him what he was trying to say.

Again, I mentioned his name. He mumbled the same thing. I stopped and asked him what he was trying to tell me. His mother said, "He is saying 'Buzz Lightyear.' He wants to be called Buzz Lightyear from the *Toy Story* movie."

At the time, I had never heard of the movie. "Okay then," I thought. "Whatever. Be flexible Doreen."

Thankfully, I did not have to use his name again. However, the groom still had to get down on his knee and speak to the boy about being his new father.

He started out, "You know, [child's name]…"

The boy interrupted, much louder this time, "Buzz Lightyear!"

The groom proceeded, "Okay, Buzz…"

When the ceremony finally came to a close, relief set in. I still wonder why the couple never mentioned anything to me before the wedding. Thinking about it now, I have a good laugh.

Fortunately, I have, so far, been an adaptable marriage officiant. Many things can go sideways. You must be prepared for anything and everything.

CHAPTER 1

What to Ask Your Partner Before You Get Married

I designed and taught the course Preparing for Marriage – Creating Your Own Wedding Ceremony, which included questions couples may consider before marriage. Some of these questions require careful consideration. Take your time:

1. What will marriage offer me that I do not have now?
2. Do we listen carefully to one another?
3. Are there things I feel I cannot talk to my partner about?
4. Do I feel there are necessary changes to be made in our relationship before we marry?
5. Do we have different expectations of one another after marriage?
6. Are we good at compromising with each other?
7. How will we split house chores?
8. Do our spending habits coincide? If not, how will we compromise?
9. Will we follow a budget? Will we have separate bank accounts?

10. How much time apart are we willing to allow each other to be with our own friends?
11. Do we want children? If so, how many?
12. What if I want to be a homemaker who stays at home to raise children?
13. Will our children follow a certain religion, or have no religion?
14. Will our children go to a public, private, religious or language-oriented school?
15. Will we tolerate and be respectful of each other's family?
16. How will we share leisure time to keep our marriage vibrant?
17. If one of us obtains a dream job in another city or country, would the other be willing to drop their position and come along?
18. If I lost or quit my job and could not find another one right away, or wanted to go back to school, would you willingly support me?
19. Will we seek out a marriage counselor if we see our relationship is becoming troubled?

Anecdote 3

The Delusional One

An acquaintance asked me to solemnize his daughter's marriage. I am honored when friends, family or acquaintances trust me to do a good job. I willingly accepted the request. I had never met his daughter and was looking forward to the proceedings because her father was such an interesting man.

During my meeting with the couple, I discovered the fiancé was not yet divorced, but they still wanted a marriage ceremony. I said that was fine, but I would not pronounce them married. Instead, I could say, "I pronounce [so and so] as loving partners in life." They seemed to agree. The wedding plans proceeded.

We visualized the entire ceremony. The future groom was quiet, agreeing with everything his future bride said. It was to take place in a large park. The bride told my husband and me that we should get there early since the two big car lots would fill up fast. She was expecting hundreds of people.

Grant and I arrived earlier than usual. The car lots were almost empty. We wondered if we were in the right location. My acquaintance, the bride's father, directed us to where the wedding was to take place. There were thirteen of us present, not the hundreds we anticipated.

My usual routine is to first see the bride and groom to make sure nothing has changed. The couple had changed their minds.

They insisted I pronounce them husband and wife in front of friends and family. I reiterated I could not legally do that. They both got upset and threatened that if I would not do it, they would get a friend who was at the wedding to perform the ceremony. Although stunned, I politely told them to go ahead. Resentfully, they stomped off. I waited and wondered.

Time passed. I suppose they spoke to their friend – who knows? They returned with no apology and no explanation, and told me I could perform the ceremony.

All went tolerably well, considering the tension (mainly mine). No one else seemed to be aware of what had transpired. The bride and groom seemed remarkably relaxed.

After the ceremony, the bride invited all of us back for the reception. She again stressed that we get there early because so many people would be arriving and it would be difficult to find parking. Leisurely, Grant and I meandered to the reception, unconcerned about parking.

Ten or twelve vehicles were parked. The crowd had swelled to about twenty. We walked into a full-sized hockey arena. We thought others must be coming later. No one else showed up. I realized this woman suffered delusions of grandeur. We stayed awhile socializing and munching on the enormous amount of food available, then left.

Next time I saw the father I asked why he did not inform me ahead of time that his daughter had "issues." He did not have an answer, other than wishing for her happiness.

Anecdote 4

Whatever!

The couple were happy with the ceremony I wrote for them, except they wanted to write their own vows. I like this because it adds an intimate, personal touch to the ceremony. They were too shy to read the vows to each other out loud. They asked me if they could repeat them after me. I agreed but mentioned that vows should not be long. If they were repeating short sentences after me, it would soon feel too long.

A week before the wedding I received their vows – almost a full page each. I called to reiterate that they might find it tedious repeating so much after me. I was also thinking of the audience. However, they wanted to leave the vows as they were. Who was I to argue?

The day came. It was a sophisticated crowd at the city's main art gallery. A string quartet from the symphony was softly playing in the background.

Time for the vows. I began with the groom. He managed to get through them with some effort. Phew! Now for the bride.

One third of the way through, I could see her frustration mount. I smiled and continued. Two sentences further, she blurted out, "Oh whatever!"

I whispered to her, "Let's finish off with the last sentence."

She agreed. We were both relieved. The rest of the ceremony went off without a hitch.

CHAPTER 2

The Marriage Officiant

THE ROLE OF THE MARRIAGE OFFICIANT

There cannot be a marriage without a marriage officiant. The officiant is appointed by the government and performs the following duties:
- prepares the marriage license
- works with the couple to visualize the steps of the ceremony
- either provides a suitable written wedding ceremony or helps the couple create their own
- is the official witness who solemnizes the marriage
- pens the final signature on the marriage license
- sends the license to the designated government department

HOW TO SELECT AN OFFICIANT: WHAT TO ASK

In general the provincial or state government provides a list of marriage officiants. In Canada, the list is found under Vital Statistics. In the United States, the list is found under Recognized Marriage Officiants by State. The list usually is found under marriage officiants or marriage commissioners.

Normally the only information listed is an officiant's full name, phone number and the languages spoken.

Rather than simply selecting names at random, you might try recommendations from friends or acquaintances. Choose a few marriage officiants and ask them several pertinent questions, such as:

1. How soon can you marry us?
2. Are you available on a specific date?
3. Are you traditional or flexible regarding a wedding ceremony?
4. Will you perform a secular marriage?
5. Will you perform a religious marriage?
6. Are you willing to say a religious prayer?
7. Are your ceremonies gender neutral?
8. How much do you charge? (The cost should be much less for a wedding in a house versus a large, elaborate wedding in a hall. A rehearsal usually adds to the cost. Mileage is also a consideration. The amount charged normally falls within suggested government guidelines.
9. How many years have you been doing this? Do you have references from couples you have married whom we may contact?
10. What documents do we need to get married?
11. How many months in advance can I get our marriage license? Where do we obtain it?
12. Can we meet you in advance of the wedding? If so, what should we bring?

13. Are you prepared to come to a rehearsal? If yes, will it cost more?

After talking to a few officiants and hearing their answers to your questions, you should be prepared to make a suitable choice.

THE MARRIAGE LICENSE

The procedures for obtaining a marriage license and marriage certificate can vary between jurisdictions and change over time.

After choosing your marriage officiant, apply for a marriage license. You can obtain a marriage license through a government office (there is a fee). Canada also has a list of marriage license issuers.

You will need:
- the marriage date
- if previously married, proof of present marital status, such as divorce decree or death certificate (if widowed)
- proof of identification with two pieces of I.D. per person (at least one per person with photo)

There is a 24 hour waiting period between receiving the Marriage License and becoming legally married. This is a period for reflection.

After the marriage is solemnized, the marriage officiant will send the signed marriage license to the government to be processed. After this, you may apply for a marriage certificate (additional cost). This is especially important if you are planning to change your name. You will need the marriage certificate to prove that you have changed your name when updating your bank accounts, credit cards, social security card, driver's license, and passport.

MEETING WITH THE OFFICIANT

Even if your marriage is occurring shortly after the required twenty-four hours, following receipt of the marriage license, try to meet at least once with your marriage officiant beforehand to fill in the marriage license and talk about your plans.

The marriage officiant should show you a variety of ceremonies to choose from that will include the impediment, vows, rings and pronouncement (the impediment is a formal request for any objections to the marriage from those in attendance). Remember you can write part or all of your own ceremony. The marriage officiant should help you visualize the ceremony from beginning to end. See Chapter 3 – The Marriage Ceremony.

Things to decide for the ceremony when you meet the marriage officiant:

1. Who will carry the rings? It can even be a pet.
2. Where the bride and groom will stand: facing each other, the audience, the marriage officiant or another variation?
3. Who will walk down the aisle with whom, and in what order? There are many variations possible. Some to consider: only the bride, the bride and father, the bride and mother, the bride and groom, or the bride with mother and father. It can be whoever you want.
4. Will the bride be given away (an old tradition)? Another option is for the marriage officiant to ask the parents

of both sides, "Who supports this couple in marriage?" The parents stand and say, "We do."

5. What will be on the signature table and how will it be set up?
6. What will the pronouncement be? For example, "I pronounce you: husband and wife, partners in marriage, loving partners in marriage, partners in life, Mr. and Mrs. _____," or another variation.
7. What will the married couple and the wedding party do after the ceremony is over?
8. Who will tell the audience what to do after the ceremony? It could be either the best man, maid of honor, marriage officiant, or someone else.
9. What music will be played and at what intervals? Typically, there are three intervals:
    a. when the wedding party comes down the aisle
    b. during the signing of the marriage license
    c. after the couple has been pronounced married and they walk back down the aisle
10. The marriage officiant is usually responsible for signaling the person in charge of music when to play each piece.
11. Will there be a rehearsal? If so, arrange a time and place.

Besides focusing on the marriage ceremony itself, you will likely discuss other parts of your wedding with the officiant. See Chapter 4 – Planning the Wedding.

APPLYING TO BE A ONE-TIME MARRIAGE OFFICIANT

In Canada and in certain states in the U.S., citizens eighteen years of age or older can apply for special permission from Vital Statistics for a one-time opportunity to perform a marriage. You must prove you are a resident and are proficient in the official language. Then you fill out the application form and send in the fee (likely about $100). The government will send confirmation of your one-time officiant license.

APPLYING TO BE A PERMANENT MARRIAGE OFFICIANT

To become a regular marriage officiant, you must be a citizen eighteen years of age or older and prove you are a resident. You must have proficient command of an official language of your state or province. Usually you can only officiate weddings in your own state or province, unless you receive special permission from another state or province.

To apply in Canada, you need to write a covering letter of introduction, and provide a current resume with two letters of reference attesting to your ability to perform the required duties. In the U.S., it is always important to check with the local marriage license office to obtain the procedures for being recognized as an officiant, as each state/county can be different.

Fees may apply in both countries, and a government training program may be required.

Anecdote 5

Wedding Faux Pas

Western boots, tight jeans and cowboy hats were the costume of choice for this western-themed wedding full of strapping dudes and gals. Lots of swaggering hips and brawn strutting their stuff. A fun scene. The groom was a handsome muscular cowboy, his bride as blond and buxom as Dolly Parton (well, almost). Both my husband and I chose to play it straight.

This was the second wedding I ever officiated. I was nervous. Before performing, I always try to find my "professional calm." It usually comes to me before I go up to face the audience. I know this is my duty. I must do it right.

I tried my best, but this time I made a slight mistake. I asked the bride, "Do you take this man to be your loving wife?"

Silence pervaded the space for what seemed like decades. Then, thank goodness, laughter. I quickly corrected my error with an apologetic smile and finished the ceremony without a hitch. I was devastated. Could they forgive me?

Later, alone with the bride and groom, I apologized for my inexperience. They laughed it off, saying it would be a memorable moment. It still is for me!

Anecdote 6

Wedding Refused

It was to be a Star Trek-themed wedding. The ceremony was taking place in the planetarium. The press would be there to record the event.

The couple wanted me, the marriage officiant, to wear a Star Trek costume. Everyone else in the wedding party would be in costume. I take my officiating seriously. I told them I would not wear a costume. They were disappointed but accepted that I would not wear one.

I discovered the fiancé was not divorced yet. He said his divorce decree was pending. Nevertheless, he set the wedding date and venue before the divorce papers could arrive. He wanted to proceed regardless. The bride-to-be remained quiet, leaving arrangements up to him. I said I could perform a ceremony for them but could not pronounce them married since it would not be true. He expected me to pronounce them husband and wife. Since the press would be there, he wanted it all to look authentic. I told them I would think about it.

There was something that did not seem right about the whole thing. I went home, thought about it, then called the couple to say I could not, with a clear conscience, perform the ceremony. He was disappointed, upset, and sounded desperate. The ceremony was only a few days away. I felt a little bad for them, but could not do it.

A few days later there was a large photo of the couple in the major local newspaper with a half-page write-up of the "wedding". The marriage officiant was in a Star Trek outfit and the ceremony took place.

Anecdote 7

No Marriage License?

A friend told me she had received permission to be a marriage officiant for a day, for a friend's wedding. (See Chapter 2 for more information on applying to be a one-time marriage officiant.) She was delighted by the opportunity. The marriage was to take place at a cottage two hours outside of the city.

She called me to ask for advice. I gave her some sample ceremonies and procedures to follow, including filling out the marriage license after the couple obtained one. I also told her to meet with the couple to go over all the details, and to get the marriage license to keep until the wedding day.

When she asked to meet with the couple, they said they were too busy. So they talked on the phone, sorting out details. The couple said they would bring the marriage license to the ceremony.

When my friend arrived, she asked the bride for the marriage license. The bride looked bewildered. Eventually it dawned on her that she had forgotten the document, two hours away in the city.

My friend had two choices: either marry the couple when they got back in the city or perform the ceremony now. If now, to make the marriage legal, she would have five days to get the marriage license signed and sent to the government to be processed.

She chose now. All else went well. The next day, the couple came to the city to sign the document.

A word to the wise: the marriage officiant should make a point of obtaining the marriage license beforehand. Leading up to the wedding day, the couple is usually very busy working on many details. It is easy to forget something; make sure it is not the marriage license. However, if it is forgotten and signed later, use the date written on the marriage license, which is the same date the couple said their vows – in other words, the day of the wedding.

Anecdote 8
N.S.F.

Someone called me to officiate a wedding, but I was already booked. I asked a new marriage officiant, who had never done a wedding, to take my place. It was a small house wedding – a good way to get her feet wet.

She agreed to take it. I gave her a few traditional ceremonies. She chose one and was excitedly on her way to solemnize her first marriage.

A few days later, she called to say the check she received for her service had bounced – N.S.F. (Non-Sufficient Funds). I was shocked. This has never happened to me. For this to happen to her on her first wedding was very unfortunate.

To avoid this situation, the marriage officiant may ask for payment in cash before the ceremony. An alternative is to call the couple, assume there has been a mistake, and say you will hold the signed marriage license until payment comes.

Anecdote 9

No Charge

My fee for a wedding depends on four criteria: size of the wedding, travel time, rehearsal or not, and if close relations (family members or friends) are involved. Occasionally I charge nothing.

The couple was from Ethiopia. They were newcomers to North America. Twelve people attended the ceremony in a very small house in a poor area of town. They were a happy lot.

After the ceremony, we celebrated with tasty, traditional food. I discovered all twelve attendees were living in this tiny house with one bathroom.

Before I left, the couple wanted to pay me. I said this was my wedding gift and left.

CHAPTER 3

The Marriage Ceremony

REQUIREMENTS

A marriage ceremony, the heart of a wedding, requires only four parts:

1. The Impediment – "If anyone present can show just cause why this couple may not be lawfully wedded, please speak now or hereafter hold your peace." The purpose of the impediment is to assess the legal eligibility of a union. I have never heard of there being a challenge to a marriage by way of the impediment (except in the movies). However, if there happened to be an objection to the marriage, it would result in a suspension of the wedding to further investigate the situation.
2. The Vows – a promise by each partner to commit to one another.
3. The Pronouncement – the marriage officiant must pronounce the couple husband and wife, loving partners in marriage, or a variation of this statement.
4. The Signatures – five signatures in total: the couple, two witnesses and the marriage officiant.

TYPICAL MARRIAGE CEREMONY OUTLINE

Tradition no longer dictates how a marriage ceremony and wedding will proceed. It is YOUR wedding. It is up to you how much or how little input and participation you want from others.

The following nine parts outline a typical marriage ceremony. Keep in mind you need not include any of this, other than the four parts noted above. Chapter 4 discusses fifteen parts of a wedding, including some of the marriage ceremony. A reminder – a <u>marriage ceremony</u> is usually only about 15 to 20 minutes and may be only a few minutes long. A <u>wedding</u> usually lasts several hours, if a celebration is to take place. However, a wedding need not be longer than the marriage ceremony itself.

1. Introduction – "We are gathered here today to celebrate the joining in marriage of _____ and _____." This is a traditional introduction. However, the introduction can begin any way you want. You might mention that this is a public celebration of commitment, and how important it is having family and friends present to help celebrate and support the couple in marriage. A definition of what love means may be added, plus the idea of two families being united to morally support the couple.

2. Readings – may be selected poems, quotes, meaningful cards or writing you have sent to each other, letters, the story of how you met, how your relationship developed and so forth. Readings are not necessary but can add a personal touch. Usually two or three readings are

inserted anywhere in the ceremony. However, think carefully how long you want the ceremony to be.

3. The Impediment – "If anyone can show just cause…"
4. The Vows – may be written by the couple to be memorized or read to one another. The couple may repeat vows after the marriage officiant or read them aloud to one another.
5. The Rings – rings usually seal the promise the couple made to each other in the vows. However, rings are optional for a ceremony. There are many reasons why either or both partners might exclude rings. For example, someone who works on heavy machinery may not want to wear a ring for safety reasons, or a couple may think it unnecessary for rings to demonstrate their commitment.
6. The Pronouncement – the marriage officiant pronounces the couple married.
7. The Signatures – bride and groom, two witnesses and the marriage officiant.
8. Benediction/Closure – kind words may be said of the couple, wishing them a long and happy life, or another reading may be given.
9. The Presentation – presenting the married couple to family and friends. "Ladies and gentlemen (or family and friends), I present _____ and _____ as Mr. and Mrs. _____ (or husband and wife), as loving partners in marriage."

To reiterate, the only parts that legally must be in a ceremony are 3, 4, 6 and 7 above. All else may be as creative as the couple wants, or eliminated entirely.

TYPES OF MARRIAGE CEREMONIES

I provide ceremonies below that I have written or gleaned from other public ceremonies. After looking at these types of ceremony, you may choose to write your own. Perhaps mix and match parts that suit you, or write your own entire ceremony with your marriage partner and, perhaps, the help of the marriage officiant.

In your readings and vows, feel free to share personal stories of how you met, cherished correspondence, or other loving moments that are meaningful to you as a couple.

This book covers nine types of ceremonies:

1. Traditional
2. Blended Families (involves children from previous marriages)
3. Wedding Anniversary Affirmation or Renewal of Vows
4. First Marriage – either Expecting a Child or With Children
5. Same-Sex Marriage
6. Double Marriage (two couples marrying separately, but simultaneously, with two separate marriage licenses)
7. Bilingual – English/French
8. Bilingual – English/Spanish
9. Bilingual – English/Italian

Only the sample script of a traditional marriage ceremony is given here. Sample scripts of the eight other types of ceremony above are found in Appendix 1 – Marriage Ceremony Scripts.

SAMPLE SCRIPT OF A TRADITIONAL MARRIAGE CEREMONY

The blanks (_____) below indicate the names of people in a specific wedding.

<u>Introduction</u>

Dear family and friends, we are gathered here today to witness the formal joining in marriage of this man, _____ and this woman, _____.

Marriage symbolizes the ultimate intimacy between a man and a woman, and this closeness should strengthen the individuality of each partner. Marriage is founded upon the most enduring yet elusive of human sentiments, love. You are not left without guidance concerning the meaning of love. It has been said, "Love is patient and kind; love bears all things, hopes all and can endure all things." In such a union you are now about to be joined.

<u>Impediment</u>

Therefore, if any person can show just cause why these two persons may not be joined in matrimony, you should declare it now, or hereafter hold your peace.

There having been no impediment declared, I ask you, _____, and you, _____, to answer the following question:

_____, do you give yourself in love and in trust to the union of marriage?

Bride: I do.

_____, do you give yourself in love and in trust to the union of marriage?

Groom: I do.

Reading

In the face of daily routine, let us discover new joy. When one feels lonely or forgotten, let us be open enough to share. May we be honest enough to express our deepest fears, trusting in each other for understanding and strength. When all around us appears chaotic, let us find peace in simple beauty. May we be bold enough to express our deepest fears, trusting in each other for understanding and strength. Amidst the haste of our busy lives, let us remember to take time to nurture our friendship and our love.

Vows

The wisdom of your hearts has led you here today. Are you ready to take your vows?

Bride and groom: Yes.

_____ and _____, please join hands and repeat these vows after me:

Bride: I, _____, take you, _____, to be my husband, to be my lover and friend, in times of joy and happiness, and in times of trial and hardship. Loving and respecting you as I do, I accept you as my husband.

Groom: I, _____, take you, _____, to be my wife, to be my lover and friend, in times of joy and happiness, and in times of trial and hardship. Loving and respecting you as I do, I accept you as my wife.

Rings

The ring symbolizes the unbroken circle of endless love. The custom of wearing it on the third finger of the left hand is said to come from an ancient Greek belief that a vein from that finger leads directly to the heart, a symbol of love and friendship. I ask that the rings you are about to exchange be regarded as a seal and a confirmation of the vows you have made.

_____, as you place the ring on _____'s finger, please repeat after me: I give you this ring as a symbol of my love and my commitment.

_____, as you place the ring on _____'s finger, please repeat after me: I give you this ring as a symbol of my love and my commitment.

Signatures (Couple, witnesses, and marriage officiant sign the registration of marriage.)

Benediction

_____ and _____, may you always communicate openly and honestly with each other. May your relationship remain one of love and trust, and may you continue to respect the individuality of the other. We hope the happiness you share today will be with you always.

To Family and Friends

Dear family and friends, you have come today to witness this ceremony. You have all shared with _____ and _____ and contributed to their growth and their happiness. It is good that you should join with them in this moment of formal commitment to each other. We ask those gathered here to accept the one as the other, respecting their individuality and their unity.

Pronouncement

Family and friends, I present _____ and _____ as husband and wife. You may kiss.

For sample scripts of the eight other types of ceremony, see Appendix 1 – Marriage Ceremony Scripts.

Anecdote 10

The Lost Ring

The wedding took place at a facility with several wedding chapels. Often three or four weddings took place at the same time. My ceremony involved the bride, groom and wedding party (including a very young ring bearer) coming down the aisle to meet me at the front of the chapel.

As the wedding party stood before me, the best man leaned in and whispered that the bride's ring was not on the ring bearer's pillow. I whispered back for him to go down the hall quickly to see if it was on the floor somewhere. Although there were many people in the hallways, I hoped it would still be there.

I slowed down my pacing before the ring portion of the ceremony came up. At the same time I considered two possibilities: change the order of events to have the ring ceremony near the end, or pretend the ring was present and go through the motions as planned (miming putting on the ring).

Miracle of miracles, the best man came back with ring in hand. He held it securely. The ring portion took place at its intended spot in the ceremony.

Another happy ending.

Anecdote 11

Wedding Theatrics

A grip asked me to officiate his wedding. A grip is a part of a production team who arranges sets and props. This grip wanted his marriage to take place in a concert hall.

He told me he dreamt of making a grand entrance. He wanted to float down from the ceiling of the theater's stage and have contemporary dancers greet him as he softly landed. They would dance around him before pitter-pattering off the stage. The bride would then walk down the theater's center aisle to meet him on stage.

"Quite a dream," I thought to myself. "Hopefully he doesn't expect me to fly in from the audience to perform the ceremony."

I told him I take my position seriously and would like to perform the ceremony in a solemn manner. He assured me that was what he wanted as well. But he felt he had to fulfill his dream. His fiancée was willing to oblige. To reassure me, he invited me to the rehearsal.

I settled into a central seat in the audience to watch the floating, dancing performance with the troupe of all young women reaching their graceful arms and bodies up to greet the groom and closing in on him as he softly landed before they flittered lightly off stage. I was apprehensive about what

I had got myself into. After the opening theatrics, I came on stage to rehearse the ceremony. It was taken seriously. I started to relax and feel relieved.

When the actual ceremony took place, I had difficulty holding back tears (one of the hazards of my job). He had a marvelous singer/friend fly in from Quebec whose voice and choice of songs were so moving, he drew us to tears. It was one of the most beautiful ceremonies I have had the pleasure of officiating.

When my husband and I were leaving, a young person came up and asked for my autograph. Graciously I obliged – the first and last time I felt like a star.

Anecdote 12

Short and Sweet

A shy and quiet same-sex couple who lived a private life asked me to perform a very short ceremony. They had been living together for many years and simply wanted the legal document. I created the shortest ceremony I could: no readings, rings, music or guests. The ceremony was held in the basement of a small community library at no cost. Perhaps it lasted all of 5 minutes.

This shows weddings can be short and sweet.

Anecdote 13

Same-Sex Marriage

Dem and Karen were well aware that same-sex marriages were not legal in May 1994. However, they wanted a marriage ceremony performed before a few friends, with two witnesses to consecrate their love and commitment to one another. I thought this was beautiful. I said I would be honored to officiate at their ceremony without the official government marriage license.

They rented a mid-sized motorboat. The ceremony took place on the river. It was a lovely ceremony. Love could be felt in the air.

Twenty-one years later, Dem and Karen called me again. They were still together. They asked me to marry them legally this time. I was happy to hear they were still partners and enthusiastically replied yes. This time the ceremony took place in their home, with a wide variety of family and friends, plus their two dogs, of course.

Same-sex marriage became legal in Canada in July 2005, and in the United States in June 2015. It was a controversial law. Some marriage officiants, including religious officiants, did not feel they should have to officiate same-sex marriages if it were against their beliefs, regardless of this new law. However, all marriage officiants appointed by the government are obliged to perform a civil marriage ceremony. Marriage officiants who refuse to perform these ceremonies lose the right to perform marriages.

In Canada, the obligation of religious officiants to perform same-sex marriages is still controversial in certain churches. In the United States, different states have different rulings: some allow religious officiants to be exempt from performing a same-sex marriage if contrary to their beliefs or religion.

When this controversial law first came in, I officiated quite a few same-sex weddings, including a double wedding. Both couples wanted to get married soon. They were afraid the next government in power might revoke same-sex marriage. This has not happened.

CHAPTER 4

Planning the Wedding

OPTIONS FOR 15 PARTS OF A WEDDING

Here are options to consider for fifteen parts of a wedding, including the marriage ceremony itself. These fifteen parts are discussed in typical chronological order.

1. Indoors or Outdoors
   If outdoors, several precautions should be taken. In case of bad weather, be sure an alternative indoor location is available that can be set up quickly. Check out the exact location where you and your partner will be standing. For example, if under a tree, be sure that sap dripping or bird droppings are not a problem. If needed, mosquito repellent should be on hand for guests. Ensure you have a heavy weight to hold down the marriage license document that sits on the signing table. Don't use a vase. I have seen a vase smash to the ground when a strong wind kicks up and the tablecloth whips around. Secure the tablecloth in some way.
   Being indoors is simpler. Nevertheless, determine exactly where you, your partner, the wedding party and the marriage officiant will stand. Plan your entrances and exits. This can be taken care of by the marriage

officiant at rehearsal, but it is advisable to plan as much as you can beforehand.

2. Musical Intervals

   Choose the pieces you want played at the ceremony. Some weddings have music playing as guests arrive, organized by a music professional or a friend. For the actual ceremony, usually there are only three or four pieces for the following moments:

   a. as the wedding party enters.
   b. as the bride enters. The person(s) in charge of music should know to fade out when the bride reaches her place. The marriage officiant can gesture as a reminder.
   c. during the signatures.
   d. during the couple's exit.

3. Readings

   Readings can be placed anywhere in a ceremony, except after the couple has been presented as partners in marriage at the very end. Typically, there are two or three readings, usually placed after the introduction, before or after the rings or vows, and after the signatures. Anyone can come forward to present the readings, or the marriage officiant can do it. You may choose to have no readings, if you want a shorter ceremony.

   See point 2 of the typical outline provided in Chapter 3 for more information about readings. A variety of readings can be found in Appendix 2 – Suggested Readings for Weddings.

4. Photography

    Get a good recommendation or two. Some photographers are procrastinators. You may not receive your photos for almost a year. Some are outrageously expensive. Decide exactly when you want the photographer to take photos – before, during and after the ceremony, during dinner and the reception? Who do you want to be in the photos? Much depends on what you can afford.

    A final but very important point, in case of serious unforeseen trouble, have at least one person take many backup photos.

5. Wedding Party Entrance

    The processional (those who walk down the aisle) often starts with the officiant followed by: groom, best man, groomsmen, flower girl, ring bearer, bridesmaids and maid of honor. Then the bride makes her grand entrance.

    However, there are many variations of the above with fewer participants. For example, the couple may decide to walk down the aisle together, or the bride may be given away (traditionally by her father). She may be walked down the aisle by both parents, or decide to walk alone. Instead of the father giving the bride away, the marriage officiant may ask, "Who supports this couple in marriage?" All parents or the entire family may rise and say, "We do."

6. Wedding Party Positioning

    Where will the couple, witnesses and the marriage officiant stand? For example, will the couple face the audience, the marriage officiant or each other? Will the couple hold hands? If so, who will hold the bouquet?

7. Ceremony Participation

    If the couple wants to involve important people in their lives in the marriage ceremony, those people can perform any part of the ceremony other than the impediment, vows, signatures and pronouncement, which must be performed by the marriage officiant (see Chapter 3).

8. Ceremony Length

    Ensure that no part of the ceremony is too long. Think of your audience (especially if there are children) and the length of their attention spans.

9. Rings

    Who will carry the rings? The ring presentation may be written by the couple or the marriage officiant. The words of the ring presentation may be repeated after being said by the marriage officiant or said to one another as the rings are placed on the third finger of the left hand. If you have a young ring bearer, be sure someone is always watching. Rings have been known to go missing (see Anecdote 10 – The Lost Ring).

10. Witnesses

    The marriage officiant will call upon witnesses when it is time to sign the marriage license. There must be two and only two witnesses who are at least eighteen years old.

11. Signatures

    Typically, a signature table is set up with one chair. In turn, the bride, groom, two witnesses and the marriage officiant sit down to sign the marriage license and registration of marriage (one document). The bride usually places her bouquet on the table, signs, then picks it up again.

12. Ending

    Once the signatures have taken place and a blessing given or a poem read, generally the marriage officiant presents the couple to the audience as "husband and wife, Mr. and Mrs. _____, as loving couple in marriage" or "the newlyweds."

13. Exits

    When the ceremony is over, what will happen? The couple may choose to walk back down the aisle. At a smaller, more casual wedding, the marriage officiant may say, "Please come forward to congratulate the bride and groom." The couple then mingles with their guests.

14. The Audience

    Usually either the master of ceremonies, best man, or the marriage officiant announces what the audience may do, such as have drinks, hors d'oeuvres, make a toast to the couple, and/or wander about the area until proceedings continue.

15. The Marriage Officiant After the Ceremony

    Once the ceremony is complete and the papers are signed, the marriage officiant leaves, unless invited to stay. It is up to you. There is no obligation to invite the marriage officiant to stay (with or without a partner).

However, this should be determined a few months before (if feasible) to give the marriage officiant notice.

WEDDING LOCATIONS – FREE TO EXPENSIVE

The choice of location might depend on the family's financial situation. If the couple and their parents do not want to spend much, a house wedding is doable and usually more intimate. Regardless of expense, the couple and family will be more at ease when the wedding is more casual and in a familiar location. This can be enhanced by getting a friend or relative to officiate the ceremony. See Applying to be a One-Time Marriage Officiant in Chapter 2.

Discussing the location with family is especially important if the couple is relying on financial support. However, it remains up to the couple to decide how the ceremony will proceed. Below is a list of venue ideas based on cost.

FREE OR INEXPENSIVE

1. Outdoors
    a. a local park
    b. a skating rink
    c. a beach
    d. on a boat (yours or a friend's)
    e. neighborhood street party
    f. in the countryside
2. Indoors
    a. family home or apartment
    b. at the marriage officiant's home

3. Indoors or outdoors
    a. school or university campus
    b. a cottage
    c. the place where you met
    d. at work
    e. a library
    f. local sports venue

MEDIUM PRICED

1. Restaurant (where the ceremony and the reception will take place)
2. Community club hall or center
3. Your church and hall
4. Short-term rental (such as Airbnb)
5. Hotel hall rental (two or three stars)
6. Museum or planetarium
7. Professional baseball diamond (a game to be played afterwards). Usually the bride throws the first pitch. Hot dogs can be served throughout. The reception may be at another location after the game.
8. A rented bus (especially if you met on one)

EXPENSIVE

1. Golf and country club
2. Private club
3. Hotel hall rental (four or five stars)
4. Banquet hall
5. Convention center
6. Yacht club

7. On an island with hired boat to transfer the guests back and forth
8. Destination wedding (often to Mexico, for the ceremony and honeymoon). I have officiated weddings before the couple went to Mexico. They wanted to be sure they were truly married with a legitimate marriage license from their own country.
9. Professional sports venue (full rental)

11 PRECAUTIONS TO PREVENT THINGS THAT MAY GO WRONG

The following are precautions I have learned to go over with couples and other marriage officiants.

1. Sometimes the wedding guest list becomes too long. The bride and groom have difficulty cutting it back, not wanting to hurt anyone's feelings. Decide on your criteria ahead of time and stick to it. For example, limit your list to close family, friends, colleagues and neighbors. People will understand you are trying to keep the guest list at a manageable number.
2. Know the details of your wedding venue and how things will be set up for the ceremony. Consider seating capacity, entrances and exits, private rooms for the bride, groom and wedding party to prepare, extra costs, and parking.
3. Have contingency plans for problems such as heavy rain, venue cancellation, a sudden illness in the wedding party, torn or stained clothing, etc. Panicking never

helps. Think of alternatives with the help of your family and wedding party.

4. Before you visit the marriage officiant, decide on witnesses, best man, maid of honor, ring bearer, and who will walk down the aisle with whom.

5. Make sure the marriage officiant knows how to pronounce your names.

6. If not paying by cash in advance, give the marriage officiant a check post-dated to the day of the wedding so you don't have to think about this detail on the wedding day.

7. Select your music and who will play it.

8. Select your photographer (preferably with references) and have at least one backup photographer in the audience.

9. If creating your own vows, rehearse them or have them written out. If they seem too long, edit them. Timing how long it takes to read the vows may be a good idea.

10. To prevent distraction during the ceremony, only introduce alcohol after the ceremony has taken place.

11. If you are making any changes such as time or location, be sure to let the marriage officiant know well ahead of time.

Anecdote 14

Popcorn Wedding

The couple was young, impulsive and obviously in love. They wanted to get married outdoors at a well-known historic venue. They had booked the spot.

I told them well in advance to have a contingency plan in case of rain. However, being in love, the sunshine in their eyes blinded them from seeing the possibility of rain. It poured.

Not wanting to get their formal attire drenched, the bride and groom panicked. They could not think of what to do. Fortunately, the groom's brother happened to make artsy films and documentaries at a small local experimental movie theater not far from their reserved ceremony venue. He suggested the entire wedding party and guests move to the theater. There was no other option on the spur of the moment.

At the theater, the brother, wanting to keep spirits up, made popcorn for all. Sitting in the theater, witnessing the ceremony being performed on the stage, the audience happily munched. All turned out well; it was uniquely romantic and entertaining.

Anecdote 15

Hockey Ceremony №1 (Neighborhood Surprise)

A neighbor and friend asked me to perform her daughter's wedding ceremony. The daughter first met her fiancé at a local pub. Unknowingly, they had lived across the street from one another for most of their lives without ever meeting.

Once they discovered each other, she said to him, "Where have you been all my life!" Things they had in common included that she played ringette and he played hockey. Soon after they met, their families got together at Christmastime to play hockey outside at the local community center. However, this year would be different.

They decided to have the ceremony at the local community center. No one except the immediate wedding party was to know. They would all play hockey, presumably as usual, for an hour and a half. After an hour I, the marriage officiant, would wander onto the ice and simply stand there smiling.

When the day came, things went as planned. The players did not get it. I was in the way of their hockey game. They looked at me as if I were crazy.

Gradually, the bride and groom came forward. I asked all to gather around. Reluctantly, they skated towards me, hockey sticks in hand.

As the ceremony began, there were tears of joy. It was quite a surprise. It was well below freezing. The ceremony was kept short, but effective and memorable.

Anecdote 16

Hockey Ceremony №2 (NHL Arena)

The marriage was to be a surprise. Only the couple and I knew it was to take place at a hockey arena, capacity 16,345, used by an NHL hockey team.

Under the pretense of a family celebration, both family and friends were invited to come for a skate. As the skating ended, chairs were brought onto the ice. Before going to a private space, the couple told participants to sit and wait for a few minutes.

Wearing a suit and carrying my usual wedding ceremony binder, I came onto the ice and stood before those seated. Smiling, I waited for the couple to return. Most of the audience thought I was there to conduct them in a sing-along.

Bride and groom skated out wearing hockey jerseys. The bride also wore a small white veil. It was a complete surprise. Who would expect a wedding in a huge hockey arena? Furthermore, the couple was older and had been together a long time.

Laughs and tears were shared, and the ceremony began. A lovely catered reception at a posh club followed.

Anecdote 17

Are They Really Married?

The wedding venue was a professional baseball stadium near a large, busy railway station. The bride and groom were avid ball fans and thought this would be a perfect venue. A dream come true.

The guests would arrive before the game, witness the ceremony, then have hot dogs. The bride would make a ceremonial pitch before the game. What could be more fitting? What could possibly go wrong?

I asked the couple if they would like a rehearsal and to check out the venue. Having been to many games at this stadium, they felt a rehearsal was unnecessary. Besides, it was to be a casual event.

The day came. The guests arrived at a location off field just inside the gates. When the ceremony began, trains were screeching constantly into the station. As the officiant, I found it very difficult to pause the ceremony for every train. The incessant noise became overwhelming. The bride and groom wanted to proceed despite the noise. What other choice did they have? At least the bride, groom and the two witnesses would be able to hear the ceremony.

It was a relief when it ended. We could get away from the constant din. However, audience members observing the proceedings looked at one another, shoulders shrugging, asking, "Is it over? Are they really married?"

This is another cautionary tale for couples wanting to wed and officiants solemnizing the marriage. Check out the venue to be sure the acoustics are good. If not, is a microphone available?

Everyone still had a good time eating hot dogs, cheering on their favorite team, and laughing as they still wondered if a marriage had really taken place.

Anecdote 18

Too Drunk to Listen

I went over the entire ceremony with the couple. We visualized every step of the way. The only thing we disagreed on is when the alcohol should be served. They wanted to serve drinks at 5:00 p.m. and have the ceremony at 6:30 p.m. Dinner would follow.

I cautioned against serving alcohol before the ceremony. Some people get distracted easily when they have had a drink or three. However, the couple wanted to loosen things up before the ceremony.

The day came, with drinks served at 5:00 p.m. 6:30 p.m. eventually rolled around. Time for the official ceremony. The bride and groom came forward. I asked friends and family to be seated. This took longer than usual.

The ceremony began. Voices in the background got louder and louder. I asked for silence. No such luck. The noise got even worse.

The best man got so upset he turned to the audience and, at the top of his lungs, yelled, "SHUT THE F**K UP!"

That did the trick. Though not the most calming of techniques, he certainly got a silence that would have made a church proud.

This is a cautionary tale for future brides and grooms, and inexperienced marriage officiants.

Anecdote 19

Time Shift

I arranged two weddings on the same day, at 2:00 and 4:00 p.m. I was well prepared for both. They were not far from one another – ideal.

I emailed the couples several days before their weddings to ensure nothing had changed, confirming time and place. The response from the bride from the 4:00 p.m. wedding closed by saying, "See you at 3:00 p.m."

I did a double take to make sure I read it right. Yes, 3:00 p.m.! I could not possibly be there by 3:00 p.m. It would be too much of a rush. Quickly I called the bride to let her know there must be some mistake. She had told me 4:00 p.m.

She said the time was changed. They had contacted their small party of guests to let them know and she emailed me. I told her I did not receive her email. She was upset. I said I had all her emails. There was no time change. She was adamant. I told her to send me a copy of what she sent to me. She never did.

I knew this was not my fault. I informed her that I could only make it for 4:00 p.m. Not pleased, she reluctantly accepted 4:00 p.m. and notified her guests.

The wedding was tense. The bride, groom and parents were quite cold towards me. I smiled and did the best I could under the circumstances.

A cautionary word for all couples getting married, and all marriage officiants – always double-check far enough in advance for any changes and confirm details.

Anecdote 20

My Error This Time

The wedding was to be in Selkirk, a town about 40 minutes from where I live. I had it in my head that the wedding was to take place on Selkirk Avenue, a well-known street in my city. I had not been a marriage officiant for long. I did not check to confirm details a few days ahead, like I do now.

As usual, I left with Grant so we would arrive 20 minutes before the ceremony started. When we arrived at the address on Selkirk Avenue, I finally realized my mistake. I panicked. Even by speeding, we would arrive over 15 minutes after the intended start time of the ceremony. This was before cell phones were common. If I stopped somewhere to try to use a landline, we would be even later. So we sped.

As we drove, we did not think going to the wrong address was an acceptable excuse. We decided to make up a better one – a flat tire. My husband had to fix it on the spot. Not a great excuse, but better than going to the wrong location, which is just plain stupid. Who could mix up Selkirk Avenue with the town of Selkirk?!

I walked in less than 20 minutes after start time. The bride was standing with the wedding party waiting anxiously for me in the hallway. My husband trailed in shortly after, tie crooked, looking disheveled. I am not sure if he added dirt to his clothing. He taught Drama in high school.

We began the ceremony immediately. Everyone was kind and understanding. A lovely reception followed. Phew!

CHAPTER 5

Unity Rituals

Some couples like to add a ritual to their ceremony. This may be conducted before or after the exchange of rings and vows. Usually this is some type of unity ritual.

Unity rituals involve symbolic gestures to celebrate the coming together of two people or two families. Perhaps the most common type is the unity candles ritual. Unity sand is a growing favorite. There are a variety of rituals that can be added to a ceremony. Below you will find eight types that I have personally performed in ceremonies: candles, sand, water, wine, flowers, love letters, tree planting, and tying the knot.

UNITY CANDLES

This ritual offers many opportunities to make it unique and personal to you. You can include your families as well. Lit candles in a dull room look beautiful. The only downside to this ritual is if a brisk wind is blowing, it does not work well outdoors.

Usually there are three candles, one each for the bride and groom and a third main one between them. How the candles are lit is flexible. Adapt and use whichever symbolism works best for you.

The couple may light each other's candles, and with these flames they light the main one. The merging flames represents their united energy, love and shared lives. The rest of the family may light their own candles.

Bride says: I light this candle as a symbol of my unique being and the gifts I bring to our union.

Groom: (Repeats the above sentence.)

Bride and groom: We light this candle together as a symbol of our unique partnership, and the increased energy we bring to our union.

UNITY SAND

This ritual is suitable for outdoor weddings (especially a beach wedding) and blended families. Usually there is a clear receptacle each for the bride and groom, containing their respective colored sand. A third clear container sits empty until after the marriage officiant explains the ritual. Usually the sand is clearly different colors. However, sand can be added from a favorite beach or cottage location, or where you are deciding to get married.

The bride or groom pours some of their sand into the empty container. Their partner follows, forming a colored layered effect. The couple pours their remaining sand together so that the two colors mix. This makes a striking ornamental keepsake for the couple.

The marriage officiant says:

You have committed here today to share the rest of your lives with each other. This relationship is symbolized through the pouring of your individual containers of sand. One represents the bride – all that you were, are, and will ever be.

(The bride pours some of her sand into the empty container.) The other represents the groom – all that you were, are, and will ever be. (The groom pours some of his sand into the empty container.)

As these two containers of sand are poured into the third, the sand in the individual containers will no longer exist, but be joined as one. (The couple pours the rest of the sand together into the main container.)

These sands can no longer be separated and symbolize your unity in marriage.

UNITY WATER

Much like unity sand, this ritual blends two colors into one. Experiment with colors beforehand so that the mixing gives a color you like. Unlike the sand ritual's individual and blended layers, water fully mixes.

UNITY WINE

Again, this ritual shows a merging of two into one by two wines being blended into one (possibly red and white wine). Then the couple drinks from the shared container. This sharing is symbolic of togetherness.

The marriage officiant says:

This cup of wine symbolizes the cup of life. It can be bitter. It can be sweet. By sharing it, you undertake to share the bitter as well as the sweet moments of your life together.

UNITY FLOWERS

Roses are a traditional symbol of love. However, you need not use roses for this ritual. Use any flower that has a special meaning to you. Perhaps use evergreen to symbolize undying love.

The couple each has a flower, as does every family member the couple wishes to include. The flower for the family members may differ from that of the couple. The bride and groom exchange flowers before placing them together into a vase. Then the family members follow.

UNITY LOVE LETTERS

The couple write love letters to each other and bring them to the ceremony. These are sealed in a box with a bottle of wine and glasses, ready for later in the marriage, such as a milestone anniversary.

TREE PLANTING

Gather two pots of dirt, perhaps from a significant place, and plant a tree in the combined soil. Family and friends may be included. You can see the tree grow as your love and married life does. You must nurture it to keep it healthy. The hole may be dug beforehand and the couple moves the tree into place and adds their dirt.

TYING THE KNOT

Usually takes place at the end of the wedding ceremony as a final promise to one another to bind their lives together. Using vines, cord, rope or ribbon, the couple's hands and wrists are tied into a knot.

Anecdote 21

At the Last Minute

A couple wanted to write their own ceremony. I gave them information regarding the necessities and let them go at it. They were both intellectuals. I trusted they could do it on their own. I asked to see a copy of the written ceremony before the wedding, so I could rehearse it before the wedding day.

Close to the big day, I still had not heard from them. I called. They said the ceremony would be finished soon. No need to worry. However, I did fret when the day came, and I had no written ceremony.

My husband, Grant, and I arrived 30 minutes before the start, a bit earlier than usual, to obtain a copy of the ceremony. It still was not finished! It was very, very, long… and rambling. They did not seem to know how to shorten or finish it. They seemed stunned.

It was now 20 minutes before the wedding was to begin. Guests were streaming in as I searched for my "professional calm." Grant, a high school English Literature and Writing teacher, offered to edit and clean it up. The couple were grateful.

I went into the hall and greeted guests, trying to stall for time, which was quickly running out.

Time was up! The ceremony was still not complete. Thinking quickly, I announced we would wait another 10 minutes as more guests were expected. Grant finally finished editing. We were ready to begin.

The written ceremony was still a little long, but it went over well. The bride and groom were happily married. Both Grant and I were happily relieved.

Anecdote 22

Marriage Tension

She was Jewish. He was not.

The bride-to-be was so in love she insisted on marriage, regardless of strong family objections to marrying a gentile. She realized her parents might never forgive her. The couple faced much tension. She was uncertain whether her parents would even attend.

As a marriage officiant, I wanted to ensure they were serious about marriage. They were not just serious, they were adamant. I shared their tension. I felt I had to be strong in supporting this loving relationship.

The ceremony was at the farm of the groom's grandmother. The appointed starting time came and went. We waited for her parents to show up before proceeding.

Eventually they arrived with the angriest, saddest faces imaginable. Tension was visible. Smiles dropped from faces and postures stiffened. I kept repeating in my head, "Professional calm."

After a tense ceremony, the bride and groom found relief by running off to have photos taken. The audience could loosen up with a drink or three. I had to leave early to perform another wedding, never knowing if there was a happy ending, like in the movies.

Anecdote 23
Biker Wedding

The ceremony was taking place on a farm. My husband and I were both invited. I met the couple earlier to go over details. We did not discuss who would attend.

Arriving at the location, Grant and I were surprised to see so many Harley Davidson "hogs." Bikers were rumbling up in full leather attire. Might a brawl break out later? Glancing at each other, we agreed to leave shortly after dinner, before booze started to flow. Drinking had already begun before the marriage ceremony. I encouraged the wedding party to proceed as soon as possible.

After the ceremony (free of disruptions), I was spontaneously asked to say grace before the meal. I was again surprised. I did not envision bikers being spiritual. Being unprepared, I gave a simple grace off the cuff: "Let us appreciate the food we are about to receive. May it bring us joy and positive energy to share with others."

Later I was blown away when two bikers came forward to say how much they appreciated my simple, non-denominational prayer.

My husband's and my opinion changed over the course of the evening. We realized we had judged them too harshly. Actually, they were a fun-loving and gentle bunch of hog lovers.

CHAPTER 6

Sound Advice and Suggestions

The following advice and suggestions were gained during my marriage of forty-nine years and hundreds of weddings I have officiated.

1. We all have issues that need to be worked on. Working on ourselves and our relationships is important for a happy marriage and a happy self.
2. Make time to be by yourself. You might go for daily walks, listen to music, have quiet time to think things through, develop a hobby or go out with a friend. Keep some of your independence. In other words, don't be overly emotionally attached to your partner. You need to keep your sense of self within the marriage. It is easy to fuse egos. This can lead to difficulties when either or both partners need more freedom.
3. Remind yourselves frequently of the love you feel for one another, and how much you appreciate this love.
4. Crucial for any marriage, or any close relationship for that matter, are: tolerance, patience, compromise, flexibility, acceptance and respect.

5. Sometimes one or both partners have a roving eye, thinking someone else may be a better partner. Be careful. You may be bored or feel things are not going as well as you expect. If this happens, consider what needs to be changed. Weigh the pros and cons of your relationship before doing anything rash.

   An extra-marital affair may look appealing initially, but looking beyond the surface, you may see dire consequences. Also, you may see the same difficulties you have in your marriage arising in an affair.

6. If your marriage is breaking down, be willing to see a counselor. A counselor can give you different and better ways to communicate with each other and a different perspective. Counseling can succeed with some work and patience on your part.

   Some couples think seeing a counselor is a sign of weakness and are embarrassed; rather, it is a sign of intelligence. You know you are having difficulties. What better way to overcome these difficulties than by talking to an expert in the field? You see a mechanic when having trouble with your car or a doctor when you think there is something physically wrong. Why hesitate when it comes to your marriage? It may cost more money than you expect (still likely less than a car repair), but the investment could save a good marriage.

7. When things are not going as well as desired you might:
   - plan a surprise outing for your partner.
   - show your love by buying a flower, a favorite dessert, or by cooking a favorite meal.

- sit down together when things get rough and make a list of positive things you like about one another. You may also list things you both want to work on in the marriage. Ongoing open communication is an important ingredient for a good marriage. The skills you learn by this communication transfer over to other relationships.
- talk to your friends. They may be going through similar experiences. Sometimes just venting to a close friend helps.
- seek out sound advice from a wise person in your life. Perhaps a friend or relative, married for a long time, has gone through and survived rough patches.

8. Other important points to consider:
- marriage, like any other relationship, takes work. Make an effort.
- love can bring deep pain, but it can also bring great joy.
- remember, every day is a new day. Don't dwell on past hurts. Talk about them then let it go.
- many people marry their opposite, probably to gain qualities they wish they had. However, these differences may get on your nerves once you are married. It is easy to assume your own way is the right way.
- establishing values you both hold dear will provide common ground for your relationship.
- remember, because of your expectations of the other, you are half the problem. Here is where tolerance, patience, compromise, flexibility, acceptance and respect apply.

- be aware it is easier to blame your partner than to come up with sound solutions to issues.
- own up to your mistakes, outbursts, and/or mean words. Be brave and responsible enough to apologize.

Anecdote 24

Lights Out

The wedding reception of over two hundred was in a large restaurant, starting at 5:00 p.m. As the bride and groom greeted their guests in the reception line, the power went off. No lights. No electricity!

The quick-thinking best man and ushers went out to buy candles for the tables. But what to do about the food that was supposed to be served at 6:30? How to cook and warm it up? Panic set in.

It was decided to serve drinks and let people chat, hoping the lights would come on. They did not. It was a major power failure affecting a large part of the city. What now?

The best man eventually thought of going to a large home improvement store that was still open to buy two portable generators. Dinner was late. The wine kept flowing. The guests happily flowed along until the food was ready – very late, but tasty.

There always will be problems to cope with in life and in marriage. Individually and collectively our attitude towards these problems makes the difference. You can choose to be positive and think your way through, or panic and respond poorly.

Anecdote 25
Best Wedding Gift

A neighbor asked me to officiate her daughter's wedding. I met the young couple at my house. They chose one of the ceremonies I had. However, they decided to write their own vows, which they would read to each other.

I said, "Sure," but I wanted a copy of the vows before the ceremony in case, at the last minute, they were forgotten, or the couple got cold feet and wanted me to read them.

I waited, then called for the vows, but never received them. As the wedding neared, I called again to see how the couple was doing with the vows. The bride sounded nervous. She said she was having difficulty finding the best wording to express herself. This made me nervous as well. She told me not to worry. The vows would be ready. I never did see the written vows, which made me more apprehensive.

The wedding day arrived. I brought some generic vows just in case. When the time came for the vows, I was pleasantly surprised. Tears trickled down my cheeks.

Their vows explained that the groom needed a kidney. The bride was willing to donate a kidney, but hers was not a match for him. He would have to search elsewhere. They found a Match Program. If the bride donated her kidney to someone else, The Match Program would find a kidney for the groom. Both matches were successful.

How romantic can you get! Tears flowed in the audience. Who could ask for a better wedding gift.

Anecdote 26

Love During COVID-19

She regularly attended a weekly evening yoga course that I taught. In fall 2018, he started coming. He moved his yoga mat beside her. In 2019, they started dating. She was thrilled and much in love. I told her if she ever planned on getting married, I could officiate her wedding.

In late 2020, she called, asking if I would perform her ceremony. Gladly I said yes. It was more romantic for me knowing they had met in my class. However, the COVID-19 virus was in full swing. We were in a Code Red lockdown. No more than five people could gather and not on personal property. The wedding party would be the bride, groom, two witnesses, and me.

The couple were outdoorsy and athletic. Both liked hiking, running, snow shoeing and skiing. The marriage would be outdoors in December, a cold month. The wedding location was one of their favorite romantic outdoor spots, far from the city. She bought a white parka especially for the occasion.

A week before the ceremony was to take place, the bride's mother died of the COVID-19 virus. The bride was devastated. She postponed the wedding to grieve. She could not stop crying. She and her mother were very close. We postponed until the new year.

The couple married in early January 2021 at the planned location. It was a lovely romantic scene in a pristine and natural environment. The future looked positive in the midst of a devastating pandemic.

CHAPTER 7

Marriage Testimonies: More Than 50 Years of Retrospection

The following testimonies were written by acquaintances I have known for years. Also, I have included my own. They demonstrate how different couples adapt and settle into a life together.

WENDY'S TESTIMONY

Currently at age sixty-seven (born 1952), I am a strong proponent of marriage, despite the social justice movements that I have engaged in over the years. They denounced marriage as an institutionalized systemic form of oppression that has its colonial roots in men's ownership and exclusive use of women's labor and bodies. I agree with this analysis. However, in the course of my day-to-day reality and in practical terms, marriage has brought me steady love, deep intimacy, soothing companionship and comforting security for most of my life.

I was engaged to be married at age fourteen. After five years engagement, I got married at age nineteen. My first marriage ended when I was twenty-four. It was a very passionate and romantic marriage, reminiscent of idealized young love. It was about a forbidden love, a deep yearning to be together, and a testament to the sheer determination of young love to overcome all obstacles. I have no regrets about that marriage and do not see it as a mistake. Most of my memories of early engagement and marriage years are filled with fondness and recollections of high adventure and insightful self-discovery that lasted a lifetime.

I was engaged to be married a second time at age twenty-nine. We married less than four months later. This time, I married a friend. The high passion and romance experienced in my first marriage was not present. In its place was a more mature and steady love that did stand the test of time. We are still married.

My husband and I are polar opposites in many ways, but it works for us. We are not tied at the hip, for one thing. Though we spend a lot of time together, we also spend time apart. My husband is a homebody. He likes routine and staying put. I am the adventurer. I like going out with my friends and going on trips. So, we do part ways regularly and then get back together to share any new happenings or experiences.

My husband is a conservative thinker. I am not. That makes many lively conversations and the occasional debate on issues of the day. We generally agree to disagree on some matters. But what keeps me in the marriage is his enduring love and kindness shown to me on a daily basis. He happily brings me coffee every morning and serves a happy hour drink upon request before dinner. He reminds me to take my pills and drink enough water. He listens to me with an open heart when I am sad about something. He cuddles up warm with me each and every night. You need to consult with him about what I offer to him in return, but he assures me that my contributions to the marriage are also substantive and appreciated.

We did adventures together over the years. We ventured out on a few multi-month bicycle trips to the South Pacific, Europe and North America. We winter in Mexico together most times, although I have traveled there several times on my own as well.

In 1990 we went to Romania to adopt two babies, one of the biggest joint adventures and challenges of our lives. Raising those two kids was a major test of our compatibility and commitment to each other, and of our ability to weather the storm over the long haul. We did it!

There are many problems with the institution of marriage but, for me, I like it. I chose it for my life. I was a marriage officiant for twenty-five years. I have performed over seven hundred weddings. I would not have done that community service work had I not believed in the institution of marriage. I support marriages for all sexual orientations. I see marriage as an important public ritual that has its roots in proclamation of love and commitment to another person as their chosen life mate. I understand some marriages do not last forever, but the intent going in is a lifetime commitment. I do not view broken marriages as a mistake, just as another lesson in life.

Marriage never lasts forever in any regard, whether it be due to death or parting ways for other reasons. I support those who do not choose marriage for their life. However, for me, marriage has contributed a lot to my happiness.

KENN'S TESTIMONY

I met my wife to be, Babe, in March 1991, one year after she emigrated from the Philippines. It wasn't love at first sight. She was not impressed with my dowdy clothes and scruffy shoes. I suppose it became love at third or fourth sight. Neither one of us were spring chickens. She was forty-nine and I was fifty-six. Parking under a bridge one evening moved things along.

I helped Babe learn to drive. As a rule, I don't recommend teaching driving to your girlfriend or wife. It could end things. Later Babe was able to total two of our cars, not always her fault. So, I resolved that when the time came to get rid of the car, I'd just turn it over to Babe.

After several years, Babe eventually moved in with me. The subject of marriage came up. People, especially the religious ones, urged us to marry. A few things held us back. My shyness and the prospect of a wedding ceremony terrified me. She was Roman Catholic and I was Pentecostal (one of those hated Protestants). Where could we get married? I suggested a civil marriage, but she would have none of it.

By the summer of 2012, I had mellowed a bit and was in the habit of saying "Why not?" whenever Babe asked me for something.

She popped the question, "Why don't we get married?"

I said, "Why not!"

I met the priest, Father Sam Argentiano, and got to like him. His great sense of humor, his broad mind and New York accent won me over. The wedding took place in September 2012. The folks on my side didn't appear to give a fig.

I have learned a few things, besides letting Babe win arguments. One is patience. I spend much of my life waiting: waiting for her to come out of the house when we are going somewhere and waiting for her to finish shopping. It always seems longer than we anticipated. I used to lose her in shopping malls or big stores. Places like the clothing section in mall shops were problematic. Babe is not tall, and the dresses and coat racks were higher. Within seconds she could lose herself for an hour. Fortunately for me, many of these shops have gone out of business.

Often the things we argue over are quite trivial. I can't remember most of them. She is always on my case to tidy all my books and files. I somewhat dread the days when she vacuums. I believe she loves to vacuum and uses the vacuum cleaner as a sort of weapon on me – to force me into at least clearing the floor of my debris.

A further word about her driving career. Driving home on the highway, I noticed the car was wandering over to the right. I looked at Babe and horrors, she was sound asleep. I yelled and, from the passenger seat, coaxed the car back onto the highway. From that time, I do most of the highway driving. When Babe drives, I don't need coffee to keep me awake.

I'm amazed at how quickly she can go to sleep. I'll be telling her something, or reading something to her in bed, and in mid-sentence she's out, while I might lie there for an hour before I can get to sleep. Occasionally she has terrible nightmares and I have to wake her. She gets angry if I don't. One time she was reciting the apostle's creed.

That brings up a difference between us. She is a faithful church attender (always Catholic, of course). I have lost my interest in religion as I get older. However, I usually go because it both pleases her, and gives me fitness as we stand up, sit down, stand up, sit down a dozen times per service. I also witness the happy looks of people after church is over. I know why. They are glad it's over.

Babe is very sensitive to comments about her Philippine culture and other personal matters. I must be careful what I say, especially while driving. Otherwise I get an ear pulled. That's why my right ear is bigger than my left.

Babe is probably one of the most caring persons you could meet. Some would say she's a nagger, or reminderer – "Have you taken your pills, washed your face, brushed your teeth, drunk water with your meal, exercised…?" How many husbands get a regular pedicure and manicure and ear-hair cut on a regular basis? I can't wish for more.

I believe an important element in an enduring marriage is to share common interests. We both enjoy travel. We both enjoy photography. We have many friends in common. Two things Babe is very good at are dancing and Scrabble. Although we are from different ethnic backgrounds, bridging our cultures has not been difficult. In fact, it has been quite enriching. As we get older, there are fresh challenges. Dealing with these is all part of staying married.

When I happen to meet Father Sam, he frequently quips, "Oh, I see you are still together." I say to him, "It's because you did such a good job."

DARLENE'S TESTIMONY

I met Bob in December of 2009 when I had moved back to my hometown after a few years living elsewhere. I had purchased a home that had a great yard with lots of potential (I am an avid gardener), but the house was dated and needed renovation. I had big plans for changes, but in the meantime, knew I had to do an immediate fix-up to the bathroom, which looked tired and depressing.

I happened to visit a friend from my previous life in what was the original farmhouse in the area. It had been moved to an historic riverbank many decades previously. I marveled that her new kitchen had all the modern conveniences but looked – somehow – as though it had always been in the house, though I knew it was a total refit. She had designed it. The contractor she used for many of her fix-up jobs had implemented her ideas. I wondered if he might be available to upgrade my bathroom. She said he was nearing retirement, but he might consider a small job such as mine was. She promised to contact him and see if he was available.

When this tall, handsome and energetic man rang my doorbell to review the job requirements, I was certainly surprised. My friend had said he was sixty-five (to my sixty-three) and – stereotypes haunting even me at my age – I had assumed he would be, well, elderly (though of course I would never have put myself in that category). He set to work with vigor. As I was working from home at my consultant's job, we had a lot of renovation-related contact over the few weeks it took to complete the bathroom. Now, Bob was married and very attached to his wife, who was ill. Our association was purely professional. Honest!

Approximately a year later, Bob's wife died. I called him to offer condolences, but didn't see him again until a year and a half later, in August 2012. A strange car pulled into my driveway and here was Bob once more ringing my doorbell, this time with an offer to "go for ice cream." I had just come in from doing a hot, nasty job of trimming grape vines and was more than surprised once again. After a quick cleanup and change of clothes, we ended up on a long drive. We found we enjoyed each other's company very much.

Well, one thing led to another. Our time together that fall passed very pleasantly. Bob was planning to spend the winter in Arizona. He mentioned the idea of my joining him there, which I assumed would be for a short visit. Imagine my surprise – yet again – when he very formally said, "I am hoping Cassie and you will come with me."

Cassie was my beloved Labrador retriever. Bob later admitted he realized that there was no chance I'd agree if Cassie wasn't included (he knew me well by then it seems!). In shock, I blurted, "For the whole time???" – which he confirmed was his offer. I told him I'd have to give it some thought over the weekend.

The rest, as they say, is history. The three of us spent a lovely winter in Arizona and our relationship flourished. Cassie also fell in love with this wonderful man. Back the next spring, traveling between two houses, we realized we didn't want to be apart. Bob proposed, I accepted, and Cassie approved. Our conversations turned to wedding plans, which we wanted to happen sooner rather than later. But who to officiate the ceremony?

As luck would have it, Bob had a great idea. One of his neighbors is Doreen Wuckert, who I also got to know through her dog, Marcie, one of Cassie's new canine contacts on our walks. Doreen told Bob she is a marriage officiant. Perfect! We would marry at Bob's home and Doreen would officiate.

So, in front of our fireplace with our friends and relatives in attendance, we said our vows on September 13, 2013. Doreen was gracious and elegant, the best possible person to lead our ceremony.

To this day we frequently meet Doreen, husband Grant and Marcie on our many neighborhood dog walks.

As for Bob and me, we are living our version of "happily ever after." Winter excursions to Arizona, a wonderful trip to New Zealand, a Panama cruise, Costa Rica, house renovations and garden development have kept us busy. We are becoming homebodies more recently. We lost our dear Cassie, but now have the wildly energetic labradoodle Tara to keep us alert, plus feral cats (now all neutered).

PAUL'S TESTIMONY

One could say we had a long courtship or a blazingly short one.

She moved in as a roommate after less than a handful of encounters. It all seemed too natural to warrant even a discussion about what it meant. We were together for three years. The decision to marry was strictly financial – we needed to move into married student housing to make it through UCLA.

Troubles we had were mostly external. She came from a family of Type As. Like all her siblings, she was a "walking wounded" from the verbal abuse of her father. She was confused by a mother she loved but found cold, distant and insensitive.

I had left home when I was fourteen and was still on a rocky road to a semblance of reconciliation with my mother. My father had been a suicide before I met my wife. We felt more or less cut off from family. Living on our own in a faraway city was part of our healing process.

We had the usual money problems in the early years. Lots of rice and beans. Several times in the last week of a month, we had no money even for food. But neither of us remember it as a stressed time. What I didn't see at the time was that both of us were fundamentally loners. Our empathy came from not finding our time apart as bad or strange.

Our first real problem came when she started graduate school. She withdrew radically and became completely immersed in her studies and research. She had a ready-made excuse for avoiding anything she wasn't interested in. The girl I had met and lived with for three years became her father: short-tempered, opinionated, careless of others, thin-skinned. I told myself it was just the strain of doctoral work. I went along, thinking I would get her back when she completed her degree. I was wrong.

Her self-isolation became more pronounced when she moved away for a two-year post-doc position in southern California. It was then I realized I was in trouble. Gradually, all things we used to do together ended. Attempts to get a dialogue going were rebuffed, each time more ferociously.

I was invited to stay with a pen pal in the Soviet Union and decided this may be a good time to start uncoupling. I handed her my ring and tried to make her understand, but could see she wasn't listening.

Russia was a wonderful time for me – I could just be myself and people accepted me. I started to think about staying. But immediately what I wanted was to share my sense of freedom and joy with my wife. I felt like I couldn't live without her. We met in Italy, but it was obvious that nothing had changed for her. She just wanted to get back to how things were.

When we got back to California, I realized I would have to build a life of my own. I started working out of town and then out of the country.

I sought counseling and came to grips with the reality that she would never change, that perhaps the closeness I thought we had in those first three years was a figment of my imagination. She is actually a kind, thoughtful person who has a very hard time empathizing with others. I don't think I've met a person more lacking in self-reflection. It made her a spectacular scientist but not an easy person to live with.

We are going through the upheaval of retirement. We have long ago developed a smooth way of living in the same space. But it has required that I tolerate self-absorbed behavior. I am not happy with my state of loneliness, but recognize that there is not enough life left to warrant making a revolution.

I now see I was doing a disservice to both of us by staying. Only by leaving would I have been any assistance to her gaining maturity and wisdom. But I just could not imagine life without her.

A long time ago I gave up on seeking companionship and closeness with her. She seems to not need intimacy of any kind. She knows almost nothing about what I do when not with her. I discovered at some point that she isn't interested, so I stopped bothering her with news about my life. It's a strange state of affairs, but one to which I have become accustomed.

I think marriage has changed me in many ways. I have learned patience and tolerance beyond anything I would have thought necessary. I have learned to respect and honor my wife's intellectual and professional achievements. I have learned to carefully separate out her many admirable qualities and keep those in mind when she is having one of her episodes. I have learned to scale back my expectations of people and accept them just how they present themselves. That has meant that I have to be decisive in identifying and getting away from toxic people. I have learned to try to "speak the other person's language," both literally and figuratively.

What I have not managed in this marriage is to hold clearly in mind what I want. I saw two counselors and came away with the same message: she would never change, and I had to decide what I wanted.

What I know now is that one needs to recognize that you marry not a person but a family. I thought the two of us were escaping together from bad homes. The moment that "real life" returns, you find you have not escaped into Lalaland but must face the families. Had I been a stronger personality, I would have and should have simply packed up and left. I spent a decade hoping that her shutting down was just a passing phase, rather than a return to life pre-Paul.

What I did wrong was to enter into a long-term relationship without having worked out, prior to marriage, what I wanted from it. There was much too much hope and way too little wisdom in how I did things.

A successful marriage is not one in which the partners are in complete sync – that leads to boredom. But the two need to be roughly under the same bell curve of lifestyles. I've watched couples go at each other over money, children, religion, family and personal traits. Marriage without differences doesn't thrive and grow. A marriage in which the partners have open communication succeeds.

My impression from our early conversations was that we would travel through life as a team and experience the good and bad together. I don't think my wife was being insincere. She just had no idea how strongly a high-pressure family experience can direct later life.

We used to have a rich repertoire of fun things to do: hike, camp, go to movies and concerts, travel, take extension courses. Now we go to concerts as often as we can, but that is about the extent of it these days. She has her projects

– gardening, knitting, chatting with her family – and I have my reading. Our paths don't cross much anymore.

One of the things that was pounded into me as a kid was that I was to keep quiet and out of sight. In my thirties, I managed to get over the pathological shyness this caused, but I never really learned the art of casual conversation. I still have a very difficult time asking someone questions about themselves. What I know of other marriages has come from observation and careful listening. Most marriages I know about have their problems. The admirable ones have a common thread: two people enjoy talking to each other and sharing experiences.

GORDON'S TESTIMONY

Ann and I have been married thirty-six years. We believe we have a successful, happy marriage. But what makes a marriage successful?

We met while at university at a painting party. I was telling people what to do. Ann thought, "Why should I listen to him? Too bossy!" (She still says that!)

We started going together. After several years we broke up. Ann taught up north. I went to study in France for a year. We still communicated, writing letters and phoning. When I came back from Europe, we became engaged. We had seven years to get to know each other and learn each other's foibles – bossiness and stubbornness, to name but two. Getting married, we were good friends and knew more or less what each wanted out of life.

We were fortunate to have good jobs and never had to worry about money. We both knew how to live on our income and plan for the future. We were able to pay off our mortgage after a few years. Ann could be a stay-at-home mom with our young son without worrying about how to make ends meet. Yes, we could have afforded a more expensive house and newer cars, but together we were happy with what we had. Many couples who make good salaries still fight about money. They often want more than they can afford and this adds to tensions.

Deaths and severe illnesses can also add stress to a marriage. These are times when a couple must work as a team with lots of support and communication.

Our early years of marriage had more arguments, usually about relatively trivial things like not picking up newspapers.

As time passed, we learned what was important to each other and arguments are now few and far between.

As a couple, we did many things together. Even with a baby at home we made an effort to get out together to do things as a couple, like going to the movies or theater, or to be with friends. Although our family is very important, it was also important that we have time together with each other.

We did many things apart. We both maintained a degree of independence. My job entailed some travel. We would have times when we were apart, then times we would travel together. I love to travel, Ann less so. We do several trips a year together, but Ann is willing for me to go off with friends or family to more exotic destinations. We both have many hobbies to keep ourselves busy.

Sleep can affect your own health and ultimately your marriage. Lack of sleep with young children can cause stress. We tried giving each other opportunities to get a good night's sleep. As we aged, periods of sleeplessness, jumpy legs and snoring made it difficult for one or the other to get a full night's sleep. Having a spare room where one of us could sleep in peace was also beneficial to our own personal well-being.

Key areas that are important for a successful marriage: having common goals that are manageable considering your joint finances, maintaining a friendship beyond the romance of marriage, balancing your independence and dependence on each other, having hobbies, doing things together as a couple and being there for each other in times of duress.

No marriage is perfect. There are always challenging times. But loving each other and discussing problems gives a good foundation for a successful marriage.

DOREEN'S TESTIMONY

I have been married to my husband, Grant Wuckert, for nearly fifty years. It is a good marriage, although we have had our ups and downs. We have known each other since December 1966. I had recently turned nineteen years old. Grant was still 18.

We met in an interesting way. A pamphlet was circulating around our city regarding Matronic, a 1966 computer program from the main university that supposedly matched couples up.

I naively thought that maybe a computer could do a better job than I was doing at meeting the opposite sex. I filled out the questionnaire and wound up with twenty-eight dates. Each one came home to meet my family before I went out for coffee with him. Grant was the twentieth date. The first time we met, we each had a good laugh. He thought I dressed old fashioned with high heels and skirt just below the knees. I was a secretary and dressed the part, the image of maturity and experience…so I thought. I thought he looked like a teeny bopper and unworldly. He wore the mod wet leather look with horned-rimmed glasses. He was the only one I went out with twice. He made me laugh more than once on that date. Just what I needed.

We seemed to be opposites. Filling out the Matronic questionnaire, he said he was atheist, I said I was Catholic. I had grade 8 education, living in a poor neighborhood. He was in first-year university, living in a relatively wealthy middle-class area. Who knew we would fall in love and marry!

The first five years of marriage were romantic and difficult. I was insecure and tended to cling. This bothered me. I did not like it nor did Grant. I never wanted him to go out with the guys or even go curling. He was patient with me because he knew I was working on it.

I started university as a mature student. I was occupied with stimulating courses, research and studying. I made new friends. All this helped me develop confidence.

Issues we initially had included spending, jealousy and tolerance of friends and family. Different viewpoints on various topics sometimes lead to arguments.

We wound up not talking to each other for a while. I later realized this was a good thing, although at the time I did not think so. It gave us time to process what happened, calm down and come up with solutions independently. However, generally I find that women tend to initiate communication. This is okay if the partner is willing to talk. Who cares who initiates, as long as both are willing to communicate?

Although there were glitches, the following years went more smoothly. Glitches should be expected in any marriage. Usually there are times when both partners will doubt whether they are with the right person. In my case, after weighing pros and cons, I knew I made the right choice.

We chose to see a marriage and family therapist when communication broke down. It was a wise decision. The therapist pointed out how we manipulate one another to get what we want, which we were unaware of. For example, I would cry and Grant would give in. Once aware of our manipulative behaviors, it was easier to change our ways. Also, the therapist showed us better ways to communicate with one another. After a few sessions, I felt we were on our way with a stronger foundation. We were more together and no longer needed her help.

Our later years together have been good, with few difficulties and many laughs. What has helped us stay together all these years is that we are both relatively flexible, empathetic, open enough to talk and willing to work things through. We also both know how to take time for ourselves. We have separate as well as common interests. All this helps us keep a happy, loving marriage.

FINAL THOUGHTS

In more than thirty years of marriage officiating, I have seen laws change to include same-sex marriages and experienced a wide variety of unusual situations. One thing has stayed consistent. Most couples still want a basically traditional marriage with vows, rings and a long-term commitment.

It has been a privilege to have officiated weddings. Seeing couples share their love and marriage with family and friends has been an ongoing pleasure for me. Grant and I had many reminiscences of our youth, love and marriage when witnessing happy couples celebrate their own. It has been fun recalling quirky moments that resulted in the twenty-six unusual anecdotes. We still have a few chuckles when we visualize some of the scenes. Despite these unusual moments, generally ceremonies turned out happily because of the love these couples had for one another, plus my great desire for things to go smoothly. I look forward to officiating marriages for years to come.

When I was young, I was skeptical about marriage. I wondered how any couple could stay together and be happy for the rest of their lives. Now I believe that, married or not, if a couple loves one another, and makes a concerted effort to make things work, likely they will have a lifetime of joy, comfort and a feeling of security and love.

This book serves as a practical guide for couples, helping provide a smooth ride into marriage. Hopefully the advice, suggestions, anecdotes and testimonies inspire readers to reflect on their own marriages and partnerships.

APPENDIX 1

Marriage Ceremony Scripts

1. **TRADITIONAL**
   Found in Chapter 3 – The Marriage Ceremony.

2. **BLENDED FAMILIES**
   (involves children from previous marriages)

   <u>Introduction</u>
   The marriage of _____ and _____ unites two families and creates a new one. The love that these two people declare today reaches out to include their children: _____, _____, _____, _____, and _____. Let us, therefore, extend to this new family our love and support. We wish you well.

   _____ and _____, you have come to this celebration with an awareness that your marriage, and the combination of your families, will have its rewards and joys, as well as its difficulties and sorrows. You have already established a strong foundation for family life. May you meet future challenges with humor, understanding and compassion. May you, by example, help your children to grow into self-reliant adults and, in turn, may you learn from them, fully appreciating their youthfulness.

Impediment

If anyone present can show just cause why these two persons may not be joined in matrimony, please declare it now or hereafter hold your peace.

Question to the Blended Family Members

Do you agree to offer love and support to each other within your newly wedded family? (We do.)

Vows

_____, do you take _____ as your husband and partner in parenthood, to love, honor and cherish? (I do.)

_____, do you take _____ as your wife and partner in parenthood, to love, honor and cherish? (I do.)

Rings

As you place the ring on each other's finger, please express your commitment to one another.

Bride:_____, I love you and will always love you. Please accept this ring as a symbol of my love and devotion to you and our children.

Groom:_____, I love you and will always love you. Please accept this ring as a symbol of my love and devotion to you and our children.

Signatures (Couple, witnesses and marriage officiant sign the registration of marriage.)

Pronouncement for the Couple
_____ and _____, you have made your vows of love, marriage and parenthood before me and all gathered here today. It gives me great pleasure to pronounce you husband and wife.

Pronouncement for the Children
You have all made vows of love, support and commitment to each other before me and all gathered here today. You are a family.

To the Couple
_____ and _____, you may kiss each other and hug your children.

Benediction
May the love which has brought you together continue to grow and enrich your lives.

Family and friends, it is my pleasure to present to you the _____ family.

3. WEDDING ANNIVERSARY AFFIRMATION or RENEWAL of VOWS

This is generally performed for a special anniversary, such as 25th, 40th or 50th, but may be anytime a couple wants to renew their vows, regardless of original wedding date.

Introduction
Welcome to the 50th golden wedding anniversary of _____ and _____, and the reaffirmation of their vows.

_____ and _____ have come here today to reaffirm the commitment they made to each other fifty years ago. They would like to express their deep devotion and love for one another in the presence of their closest family and friends.

This devotion and love have carried them through the years. Their life was never too difficult or complicated because together they resolved their problems. They had their ups and downs, but learned to communicate with each other in positive ways and with a sense of humor. They learned to appreciate each other's strengths and accept each other's weaknesses. They supported each other through the hard times. They learned to be together, but always took time for themselves and their own friends.

Their children _____ and _____ have benefited from this strong bond. They have become self-reliant, confident and responsible adults with families of their own.

<u>Impediment</u>

If anyone can show just cause why these two people may not be joined in matrimony, please declare it now or hereafter hold your peace.

There having been no impediment declared, are you ready to say your vows? (Yes we are.)

<u>Exchange of Vows and Rings (likely original wedding rings)</u>

_____, as my husband, I reaffirm that I will love and cherish you in sickness and in health, for better or for worse, for richer or for poorer, now and forever. I give you this ring as a symbol of my love and commitment to you.

_____, as my wife, I reaffirm that I will love and cherish you in sickness and in health, for better or for worse, for richer or for poorer, now and forever. I give you this ring as a symbol of my love and commitment to you.

<u>Signatures</u> (Couple, witnesses and marriage officiant sign the registration of marriage.)

<u>Benediction</u>
_____ and _____, may your marriage continue to be a shared adventure. May your love outlive you and become the inheritance of your grandchildren and their grandchildren to come. May your home be a place of love, warmth and laughter.

<u>Quote from Robert Browning</u>
Grow old along with me! The best is yet to be.

<u>Pronouncement</u>
Family and friends, I would like to present _____ and _____ as dedicated partners in marriage. You may kiss.

4. FIRST MARRIAGE – either EXPECTING a CHILD or WITH CHILDREN

Note that this first part only applies to couples who are expecting children.

Introduction

Dear family and friends, _____ and _____ are happy that you could all be here to celebrate their marriage, as well as the forthcoming birth of their child. This unborn child is a confirmation of their love. We are here today to formally recognize this loving union and support this new family.

The Charge to the Couple

_____ and _____, you have come to this celebration with an awareness that your marriage will have its joys as well as its sorrows. Your lives will be intertwined with that of _____, your child. As you have already established a strong foundation for a family life, you will be able to meet future challenges with humor, understanding and compassion. May you, by example, help your children and future children to grow into self-reliant adults and, in turn, may you learn from them, fully appreciating their youthfulness. We wish you well!

Impediment

If anyone can show just cause why these two persons may not be joined in marriage, please speak now or hereafter hold your peace.

There having been no impediment declared I ask you both to exchange vows.

Exchange of Vows

Groom:_____, I take your hand in mine. I promise to be your lover and your friend. I promise to remain loyal and honest. I take your hand in mine for this hour, for this day and for this lifetime. I am looking forward to being the father of our child and will provide for both of you the best I can.

Bride:_____, I love you. I will always love you in sickness and in health and for better or worse. I will communicate openly and honestly with you. I will do all I can to keep this marriage alive and loving, so that our children grow up in a happy and healthy environment.

Ring Ceremony

I ask that the rings you are about to exchange be regarded as a seal and a confirmation of the vows you have made.

Let the groom repeat after me:

_____, I give you this ring as a symbol of my love and friendship. As it encircles your finger, may it remind you always that you are my best friend and are surrounded by my enduring love.

Let the bride repeat after me:

_____, I give you this ring as a symbol of my love and friendship. As it encircles your finger, may it remind you always that you are my best friend and are surrounded by my enduring love.

Pronouncement

_____ and _____, you have made your pledges of marriage to the other. You have done so in the presence of all who have gathered here today. I now pronounce you husband and wife.

Benediction
May the love which has brought you together continue to grow and enrich your lives and your children's lives, bringing peace and inspiration to each of you and to those who know you.

Signatures (Couple, witness and marriage officiant sign the registration of marriage.)

Presenting the Couple
I would now like to introduce Mr. and Mrs. _____. Please join them for a glass of champagne to celebrate their happiness.

5. **SAME-SEX MARRIAGE**

Introduction
_____ and _____ feel that your presence here today is very important because each of you has, in your own way, contributed something precious to their lives.
They hope that the words they have chosen for their ceremony will help you to enjoy and become part of this special celebration.

Reading – Undreamed of Heights by Colleen Townsend Evans
In a marriage, a loving couple can discover the thrill of trusting each other so fully that their freedom of expression reaches undreamed-of heights. Their intimacy becomes a sanctuary, a place where the soul of their relationship can grow through their physical oneness.

No matter how many others they may share life within the circle of family and responsibilities, they have a small private world where they can offer each other their trust, their vulnerability, and the unrestrained affirmation of their love.

Impediment

If anyone present can show just cause why these two persons may not be lawfully joined in matrimony, you should declare it or hereafter hold your peace.

Vows

_____ and _____, please together repeat these vows after me:
I take you as my spouse, for better or for worse, to continue to share our joys and sorrows in an atmosphere of friendship and love.

Pronouncement

Now that you accepted your vows of love and marriage, I pronounce you loving partners in marriage. You may kiss.

Rings

I ask that the rings you are about to exchange be regarded as a seal and a confirmation of the vows you have made.

_____, as you place the ring on _____'s finger, please respond to the following question:
Do you, _____, promise _____ that they will be your spouse and you will stand by them

in sickness and health, in joy and sorrow; and do you pledge to them your respect and your love? (I do.)
_____, as you place the ring on _____'s finger, please respond to the following question:
Do you, _____, promise _____ that they will be your spouse and you will stand by them in sickness and health, in joy and sorrow, and do you pledge to them your respect and your love? (I do.)

Signatures (Couple, witnesses and marriage officiant sign the registration of marriage.)

Presenting the Couple
Family and friends, I present _____ and _____ as loving partners in marriage.

6. DOUBLE MARRIAGE (two couples marrying separately, but simultaneously, with two separate marriage licenses)

This ceremony is suitable for same-sex couples as well.

Introduction
We are gathered here this evening to witness the formal joining in marriage of _____ to _____, and _____ to _____.
No minister, priest or public official can marry you. Only you can truly marry yourselves by mutual commitment to love each other. Working to create an atmosphere of care, consideration and respect, and a willingness to face the tensions and anxieties that underlie human life, can make your wedded life come alive.

On this day of your marriages, you stand somewhat apart from others. You stand within the charmed circle of your love. This is as it should be. But love is not meant to be the possession of two people alone. Rather it should serve as a source of common energy.
May you come closer together than ever before but, at the same time, may your love give you the strength to stand apart, to seek out your unique destinies, to make your special contribution to the world.

Impediment

If anyone present can show just cause why these two couples may not be joined in matrimony, please declare it now or hereafter hold your peace.

Vows

The wisdom of your hearts has led you here today. Are you ready to take your vows? (Yes.)
Please join hands with your partner and repeat these vows after me:
I take you to be my partner for life, to be my lover and friend, in times of joy and happiness and in times of trial and hardship. Loving and respecting you as I do, I accept you as my partner in marriage.

Rings

The ring is a symbol of love and friendship. It is to seal and confirm the vows you have made to one another. Please place the ring on each other's finger and repeat after me:
I give you this ring as a symbol of my love and commitment to you.

(The couples can repeat the above individually, simultaneously or consecutively.)

Reading
George Eliot spoke eloquently about the essence of love. She said, "What greater thing is there for two human souls than to feel they are joined together to strengthen each other in all labor, to minister to each other in all sorrow, to share with each other all gladness, to be one with each other in the silent memories."

Pronouncement
_____and _____, and _____ and _____, now that you have exchanged vows and rings, I pronounce you partners in marriage. You may kiss.

Signatures (Couples, witnesses and marriage officiant sign the two registrations of marriage.)

Closing Remarks
Marriage is a dynamic process of discovery.
Marriage is an art. It requires active thought, creativity and effort.
Marriage is a life's work.
And now a toast to the couples.

7. **BILINGUAL – ENGLISH/FRENCH**

To the audience: The ceremony will be in English and French.
La cérémonie sera en anglais et français.

Introduction

Dear family and friends, _____ and _____ will promise themselves to each other. They wish to thank you for being present here this evening as they begin their journey together.

Chers famille et amis, _____ et _____ vont se promettre l'un à l'autre. Ils vous remercient d'être présents ici ce soir alors qu'ils entament leur voyage ensemble.

Impediment/l'Empêchement

If anyone present can show just cause why the two persons may not be lawfully joined in matrimony, you should declare it or hereafter hold your peace.

S'il y a quelqu'un dans cette assemblée qui connaît une raison juste et valable susceptible d'interdire à ces deux personnes d'être unies par les liens du mariage, qu'il fasse état de ses raisons maintenant, ou bien qu'il se taise pour toujours.

There having been no impediment declared or admitted, I ask you, _____ and _____, to join hands.

Puisqu'aucun empêchement n'a `été déclaré ou avoué, je vous prie _____ et _____ de joindre vos mains.

Vows/Voeux

_____ and _____, the wisdom of your hearts has led you here today. Are you ready to take your vows and exchange rings? (Yes.)

_____ et _____, la sagesse de vos coeurs vous a conduit ici aujourd'hui. Etes-vous prêts à faire vos voeux et échanger vos anneaux? (Oui.)

I, _____, take you, _____, to be my lawful wedded husband, to have and to hold, from this day forward, for better for worse, for richer or poorer, in sickness and in health, to love and cherish until death do us part. I pledge you my word, and I call upon those present to witness the declaration that I freely make.

Moi, _____, je te prends, _____, pour épouse légitime, pour t'avoir comme compagne dès aujourd'hui et à jamais, pour le meilleur et pour le pire, dans la richesse ou la pauvreté, la maladie ou la santé, pour t'aimer et te chérir jusqu'à ce que la mort nous sépare. Et pour cela, je te donne ma parole et je fais appel à tous ceux ici présents pour qu'ils soient témoins de cette déclaration que je fais de mon plein gré.

Rings/Alliances

In as much as you have made this declaration of your vows concerning one another, and have set these rings before me, I ask that these rings be regarded as a seal and a confirmation of the vows you have made. Puisque vous avez prononcé tous deux vos voeux réciproques et que vous avez déposé ces alliances devant moi, je vous demande de les porter et de les considérer comme le sceau et la confirmation des voeux que vous avez fait.

Bride: _____, may this ring be the pledge of my vows. I promise to be true and faithful in marriage.

Groom: _____, que cette alliance soit le symbole de mes voeux. Je te promets d'être sincère et fidèle dans ce mariage.

Reading/Lecture
Let your home be a haven of peace amidst a busy and businesslike world. Let your relationship be one of truth and understanding. Respect the confidences of your partner in this marriage. Consider that as the world gives nothing for nothing, neither will your marriage yield you more than you put into it.

Que le vôtre soit un havre de paix dans un monde bruyant et affairé; que votre relation en soit une de profonde sincérité et de compréhension mutuelle. Respectez les confidences de votre conjoint. N'oubliez pas que, comme le monde en donne rien sans rien, votre mariage ne vous apportera rien de plus que vous y mettrez.

May you enjoy length of days, fulfillment of hopes, and peace and contentment of mind as you live and fulfill the terms of this commitment you have made with one another.

Que vous soyez heureux très longtemps, en tâchant de réaliser vos espérances et en gardant l'esprit paisible et satisfait, tandis que vous vivez et remplissez chaque jour les termes de cet engagement que vous avez pris l'un envers l'autre.

Signatures (Couple, witnesses and marriage officiant sign the registration of marriage.)

Pronouncement/Prononcement
Now that you, _____, and you, _____, have consented in legal wedlock, and have declared your solemn intention in this company before these witnesses, and in my presence, I pronounce you husband and wife.
Maintenant, puisque vous, _____, et vous, _____, avez tous deux consenti à être unis par les liens du mariage et que vous avez prononcé vos voeux solennels devant cette assemblée qui en est témoin, et devant moi-même, je vous déclare mari et femme.
You may kiss. Vous pouvez vous embrasser.

8. BILINGUAL – ENGLISH/SPANISH

To the audience: The ceremony will be in English and Spanish.
La ceremonia sera en español y inglés.

Introduction/Introducción
We are gathered here today to witness the union of this man, _____, and this woman, _____, in matrimony.
Marriage is a union to help and counsel one another through good times and bad times.
Estamos reunidos aquí este día con el propósito de unir este hombre, _____, et esta mujer, _____, en matrimonio.

El matrimonio fue ordenado para crear una unión
para ayuda y consuelo mutual en ambos prosperidad
y adversidad.

Impediment/Impedimento
If anyone present here today can show just cause
why these two persons may not be lawfully joined in
matrimony, you should declare it now or hereafter hold
your peace.
Si alguien de los aquí presente puede mostrar con causa
justificada el porque estas dos personas no pueden
unirse por la ley, que lo declare ahora o que calle
para siempre.
Since no impediment has been declared, I ask you to
join hands.
No teniendo ningún impedimento que hubiese sido
declarado, yo les pido a ustedes que unan las manos.

Vows/Votos
The wisdom of your hearts has led you here today. Are
you ready to take your vows? (Yes.)
La sabiduría de sus corazones ha dirigido ustedes aquí.
Están ustedes listos a hacer sus votos? (Si.)
I ask the groom to repeat these vows after me:
I ask all here today to serve as witnesses that I take
_____ to be my lawful wedded wife, to share
our joys and sorrows in an atmosphere of friendship
and love.
Yo pido al novio que repita después que yo:
Yo les pido a todas las personas aquí que sirvan de
testigos que yo tomo a _____ para hacer mi

legítima esposa y compartir nuestra alegría y tristeza en una atmósfera de amistad y amor.
I ask the bride to repeat these vows after me:
I ask all here today to serve as witnesses that I take _____ to be my lawful wedded husband, to share our joys and sorrows in an atmosphere of friendship and love.
Yo pido a la novia que repita después que yo:
Yo les pido a todas las personas aquí que sirvan de testigos que yo tomo a _____ para hacer mi legítimo esposo y compartir nuestra alegría y tristeza en una atmósfera de amistad y amor.

The Rings/Los Anillos

The circle has no beginning and no end. The rings you are about to exchange represent the unity of your lives.
El círculo no tiene un principio ni un fin. Los anillos que ustedes dan uno al otro representan la unidad de sus vidas.

_____ (Groom), place the ring on the third finger of _____'s left hand and repeat after me:
Accept this ring as a symbol of my promise of love.

_____ (Novio, ponga el anillo en el tercer dedo de la mano izquierda de _____ y repita después que yo:
Acepta este anillo como símbolo de mi promesa de amor.

_____ (Bride), place the ring on the third finger of _____'s left hand and repeat after me:
Accept this ring as a symbol of my promise of love.

_____(Novia), ponga el anillo en el tercer dedo de la mano izquierda de _____ y repita después que yo:
Acepta este anillo como símbolo de mi promesa de amor.

Reading/Lectura
Marriage is a process of discovery.
Marriage is a journey, not an arrival.
Marriage is an art. It requires active thought, effort and creativity.
Marriage is a life's work.

El matrimonio es un proceso de descubrimiento.
El matrimonio es un viaje, no una llegada.
El matrimonio es un arte. El exige el pensamiento activo, el esfuerzo y la creatividad.
El matrimonio es una obra para toda la vida.

Pronouncement/Declaración
Now that you, _____, and you, _____, have accepted your vows of love and marriage and have declared your solemn intentions before these witnesses; and having exchanged rings as a promise of your love and confidence in one another, I pronounce you husband and wife.
Y ahora, por tanto, como tú, _____ y tú _____ han consentido en este matrimonio legal, y han declarado su intención solemne ante estos testigos; y han intercambiado estos anillos como promesa de su confianza para con cada uno de ustedes, yo los declaro marido y mujer.

Signatures/Firmas (Couple, witnesses and marriage officiant sign the registration of marriage.)

Benediction/Benedición
_____ and _____, may the happiness you share today be with you always.
_____ y _____, que la felicidad que ustedes comparten hoy, sea con ustedes por siempre.
Dear family and friends, I present _____ and _____ as partners in marriage.
Querida familia y amigos, yo le presento _____ y _____ como parejas en matrimonio.

9. BILINGUAL – ENGLISH/ITALIAN

To the audience: The ceremony will be in English and Italian.
La cerimonia sarà in inglese e italiano.

Introduction/Introduzione
We are gathered here today to join in matrimony this man, _____, and this woman, _____.
Siamo riuniti qui oggi per unire, questo uomo, _____, e questa donna, _____, in matrimonio.

Impediment/Impedimento
If any of you present can show just cause why these two persons may not be lawfully joined, you should declare it or hereafter hold your peace.

Se qualcuno è a conoscenza di un motivo per cui non si debba officiare questo matrimonio, parli ora o taccia per sempre.
There having been no impediment declared, I ask you, _____, and you, _____, to join hands.
Non essendoci impedimento, chiedo allo sposo, _____, ed alla sposa, _____, di unire le loro mani.

Reading/Lettura
Marriage is a dynamic process of discovery.
Marriage is a journey, not an arrival.
Marriage is an art. It requires active thought, creativity and effort.
Marriage is a life's work.
Il matrimonio è un processo dinamico de scoperta.
Il matrimonio è un scammino, non un arrivo.
Il matrimonio è un'arte. Richiede pensieri attivi, lo sforzo et la creatività.
Il matrimonio è un'opera per la vita.

Vows/Giuramenti
_____ and _____, the wisdom of your hearts has led you here today. Are you ready to take your vows? (Yes.)
_____ e _____, la sagezza dei vostri cuori vi ha condotti qui oggi. Siete pronti di dichiarare le vostre Intenzioni? (Si.)
_____ (groom), please repeat after me:

Groom: I, _____, take you, _____, as my lawful wedded wife, for better or worse, to continue to share our joys and sorrows in an atmosphere of friendship and love.

_____ (sposo), per favore ripeti dope di me:

Sposo: Io, _____, ti prendo, _____, come mia ligitima sposa, in tempi de prosperità e di aversita, a dividere le nostre gioie e le nostre pene in un'atmosfera de amicizia e di amore.

_____ (bride), please repeat after me:

Bride: I_____, take you, _____, as my lawful wedded husband, for better or worse, to continue to share our joys and sorrows in an atmosphere of friendship and love.

_____ (sposa), per favore ripeti dope di me:

Sposa: Io, _____, ti prendo, _____, come mio ligitimo sposo, in tempi de prosperità e di aversita, a dividere le nostre gioie e le nostre pene in un'atmosfera de amicizia e di amore.

<u>Rings/Anelli</u>

_____ (bride), place the ring on the third finger of _____'s hand and repeat after me:

Bride: _____, accept this ring as a symbol of my promise of love.

_____ (sposa), metti l'annello al terzo ditto della mano sinistra di _____ e ripeti dopo di me:

Sposa: _____, acceta questo anello come un simbolo della mia promessa del mio amore.

_____ (groom), place the ring on the third finger of _____'s left hand and repeat after me:

Groom: _____, accept this ring as a symbol of my promise of love.

_____ (sposo), metti l'anello al terzo ditto della mano sinistra di _____ e ripeti dopo di me:

Sposo: _____, acceta questo anello come un simbolo della mia promessa de amore.

Pronouncement/Dichiarazione
Now that you, _____, and you, _____, have accepted your vows of love and marriage, I pronounce you husband and wife.
Adesso che voi, _____, e voi, _____, avete dichiarato le vostre intenzioni di amore e di matrimonio, vi dichiaro marito e moglie.
You may kiss/Potete baciarvi.

Signatures/Le Firme (Couple, witnesses and marriage officiant sign the registration of marriage.)

Closing/Chiusura
_____ and _____, may your courage to love outlive you and become the inheritance of your children and their children to come.
_____ e _____, possa il vostro corragio di amare sopravvivere a voi e diventi eredità per i vostri figli e per i loro figli.

Family and friends, I present Mr. and
Mrs. _____.
Parenti ed amici, io vi presento il signor e la
signora _____.

APPENDIX 2

Suggested Readings for Weddings

The following readings frequently have been selected by couples over the years.

On Marriage (excerpts), from the book *The Prophet*, Kahlil Gibran

> Love one another, but make not a bond of love:
> Let it rather be a moving sea between the shores of your souls.
> Sing and dance together and be joyous,
> But let each one of you be alone,
> Even as the strings of a lute are alone
> Though they quiver with the same music.
> Give your hearts, but not into each other's keeping.
> For only the hand of Life can contain your hearts.
> And stand together yet not too near together:
> For the pillars of the temple stand apart,
> And the oak tree and the cypress grow not in each other's shadow.
> Let there be spaces in your togetherness,
> And let the winds of the heavens dance
> between you.

A Couple's Promise (author unknown)

> In the face of daily routine, let us discover new joy.
> When one feels alone and forgotten, let us be open enough to share.
> May we be honest enough to express our deepest fears,
> Trusting in each other for understanding and strength.
> When all around us appears chaotic, let us find peace in simple beauty.
> May we be bold enough to discover our individuality
> And wise enough to accept our differences.
> Amidst the haste of our busy lives, let us remember to take time
> To rekindle our friendship and our love.

Shakespeare Sonnet 116

> Let me not to the marriage of true minds
> Admit impediments. Love is not love
> Which alters when it alteration finds,
> Or bends with the remover to remove.
> O no! It is an ever-fixèd mark
> That looks on tempests and is never shaken.
> It is the star to every wandering bark,
> Whose worth's unknown, although his height be taken.
> Love's not Time's fool, though rosy lips and cheeks
> Within his bending sickle's compass come.
> Love alters not with his brief hours and weeks,

But bears it out even to the edge of doom.
If this be error and upon me proved,
I never writ, nor no man ever loved.

Other Suggested Readings:

"Unending Love," Rabindranath Tagore
"I Carry Your Heart with Me," e.e. cummings
"Apache Wedding Prayer," Elliott Arnold
"A Vow," Wendy Cope
A Natural History of Love, Diane Ackerman
"The Art of Marriage," Wilferd Arlan Peterson
I Like You, Sandol Warburg
Some Things Go Together, Charlotte Zolotow
"Growth Model," Virginia Satir
"To Be One with Each Other," George Eliot
"A White Rose," John Boyle O'Reilly
"Love is a Great Thing," Thomas à Kempis
"I Love You," Carl Sandberg
"The Beauty of the Trees", adapted poem by Chief Dan George
"I Love You," Roy Croft
"Our Souls Are Mirrors," Rupi Kaur
"To Love Is Not to Possess," James Kavanaugh
"The Earth Turned to Bring Us Closer," Eugenio Montejo
"I'll Be There for You," Louise Cuddon
"Variations on the Word Love," Margaret Atwood
"Touched By An Angel," Maya Angelou
"The Passionate Shepherd to His Love," Christopher Marlowe
"Sonnet 17," Pablo Neruda (translated by Stephen Tapscott)
"The Privileged Lovers," Rumi
"This Marriage," Rumi

"Chemistry," Nayyirah Waheed
"The Wedding Vow," Sharon Olds
"We," Nayyirah Waheed
"About Marriage," Denise Levertov
"Married Love," Kuan Tao-Sheng
"A Blessing for Wedding," Jane Hirshfield

APPENDIX 3

Recommended Books

The following books are helpful guides for marriage, parenthood and life in general. Some were recommended by couples I have married. Some I have learned from myself.

The Dance of Anger: A Woman's Guide to Changing the Patterns of Intimate Relationships, Harriet Lerner, PhD

The premise is: if we do not change our patterns, or take a different approach, nothing will change in our relationship. Dr. Lerner provides ideas on changing our patterns. If our partner will not change, we still can try something different for ourselves. When we make changes in our own lives, the world around us changes as well.

When Things Fall Apart, Pema Chodron

Pema Chodron, through the teachings of Buddhism, gives insights to explore our feelings to come closer to our own truth. She teaches how to stay strong by facing our pain, knowing that many others in the world feel the same hurt, and learning how to be empathetic with these others. Through a practice called Tonglen, we can move forward to make needed changes.

Comfortable with Uncertainty: 108 Teachings on Cultivating Fearlessness and Compassion, Pema Chodron

Teachings are designed to help develop our compassion and awareness amid the challenges we face in our lives. Topics include:
- letting go of what you cannot control
- letting go of what does not serve you
- mindfulness
- working through hurtful feelings
- overcoming habitual patterns that prevent us from being free and happy

After the Honeymoon, Daniel Wile, PhD

Many of us have difficulty expressing our feelings, especially feelings of hurt. Instead we become defensive. Daniel Wile teaches intimate ways to communicate, and thus learn to express bottled up pain. This can lead to a closer relationship with our partners.

Feel the Fear and Do It Anyway, Susan Jeffers

Jeffers teaches how to stop negative thinking, and to switch our brains into thinking more positively. She provides a practical ten-step approach to positive thinking.

CPSIA information can be obtained
at www.ICGtesting.com
Printed in the USA
LVHW100353220722
724080LV00002BA/27

9 781525 590856